HOW TO GET ... IN FLY FISHING

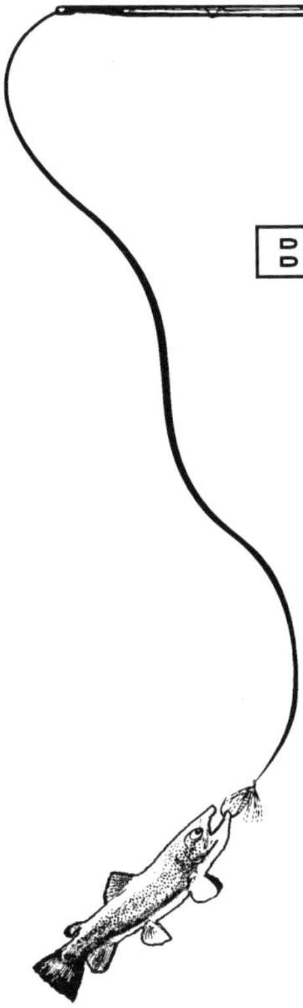

WITHOUT GOING BROKE, CRAZY, OR TO PATAGONIA

To Keith
Beginner's Mind =
Beginner's Luck
Beginner's
Fred

Written and Illustrated by
FREDERIC THORNER

With Humorous Illustrations by
LINDA TAGLIAFERRO

Visit us on the web: www.GetStartedInFlyFishing.com

FITZ HAUS
Little Neck, New York

All inquiries should be addressed to
Fritz Haus
248-44 Thebes Avenue
Little Neck, NY 11362

Cover and book design by Frederic Thorner
Illustrations by Frederic Thorner and Linda Tagliaferro

Book composition and computer graphics
by Jay Green Graphics

Printed in the United States of America
on recycled, environmentally friendly paper.

Library of Congress Control Number: 201192415

ISBN: 978-0-983587-0-7

www.GetStartedInFlyFishing.com

Table of Contents

To the memory of my father

Arnold "Buster" Thorner
who taught me many things,
most importantly, how to fish

I would like to thank the following people for their help in creating this book:

Linda Tagliaferro,

editor, proofreader, illustrator, wife and muse

Eric Thorner,

consultant, great son and great caster

Jay Green,

without whose help this book and many of my other projects would not have been possible

Betsy Jacobson,

for setting up the original formatting of the book and for many other favors

Jeff Clapp,

for his help with the cover

Walter Lynch,

for his help and patience

Paul Cimaglia,

for his production help and for being a great fishing buddy

El Kazan,

consultant, teaching partner and great fishing buddy

Eileen Dwyer, Carlisle Neblett, Mike Love and Brad Mintz

for their help and support

Brook Trout

INTRODUCTION

Getting started in fly fishing can be a daunting experience. While not as scary as sky diving or marriage, it still may manage to instill some feelings of apprehension.

Casting a fly line appears to be a difficult task requiring the agility of a tightrope walker and the coordination of a circus juggler.

Understanding the equipment and techniques involved seems just about as easy as quantum physics. Line types and weights, leaders, tippets, endless types of flies and the swarms of insects they represent add to the confusion and dismay of anyone considering embarking on this journey.

The term "sticker shock" seems an understatement. Browsing through the endless array of equipment and gadgets helps to underscore the gnawing suspicion that the cost of engaging in this activity might come to a little less than a villa in the south of France.

Exotic destinations only serve to reinforce the sense that the sport of fly fishing, like polo and big game safaris, is only for the idle rich.

Not so! This book intends to cure you of your "fear of fly fishing." It will debunk the myth that fly fishing is difficult, exotic, elitist and expensive. It will point out places to fly fish that do not require transportation by helicopter, hovercraft or Humvee.

This book is small – purposely small. Just as a good musician knows that the silent pauses are as important as the music itself and a good painter or designer knows that there must be areas within the composition to rest the eye, a good teacher knows not to overwhelm you with too much information. What I choose not to tell you is just as important as what I tell you. It's all about how much information one can digest, not just about how much is offered.

There are many more comprehensive fly fishing books out there and most are excellent. In my opinion they are more suited for intermediate fly fishers. Unless you're an Einstein, they are very likely to confuse you when you are first attempting to understand this subject. Later, after you have absorbed the basic information, there will be an abundance of great knowledge available from many sources. The study of fly fishing may be pursued for a lifetime if one so desires.

This little book is intended as a primer. Its goal is to get you started with a clear understanding of how to learn in an enjoyable way, and as the subtitle states, "without going broke, crazy or to Patagonia."

Brown Trout

WHY FLY FISH?

Although it is often perceived as complex, fly fishing is extremely simple. This is probably why it was one of the first methods of fishing. Some astute ancestors of ours noticed fish–very possibly trout–feeding on the surface of the water. Using fur, feathers or other natural materials, they created a rough imitation of the insect the fish were feeding on, tied it on a hook, put it on the end of a line, and caught fish. Soon they realized that by tying the line to the end of a stick, they could get the line out further and control it better. Somewhere along the way, they discovered that they could whip the line out even further. Long, willowy rods seemed to work best for this whipping or casting method. Reels didn't come along until much later (sometime in the seventeenth century.)

Historians disagree as to exactly when or where fly fishing began. Some say ancient Egypt, China or Greece. But they say that about almost everything. Like many inventions and discoveries, it might have happened in a couple of different places at a couple of different times. Let's just be glad it happened.

Although it takes a little skill to cast a fly line, the simplicity of the method is part of its appeal. The graceful quality of fly casting is another part. There's something intrinsically beautiful in the movements of a loop of fly line rolling through the air and landing gently on the water. There's a poetry going on there that compliments the quiet beauty of nature.

Is fly fishing more effective than other methods? Sometimes it is and sometimes it's not. There have been times when I've seen spin fishing with bait or lures outfish fly fishing as well as times when fly fishermen were killing them and spin fishermen couldn't get a tap. The reasons why fish will go for one thing and reject another are myriad and complex. So I would say it is as effective as any other method depending on the circumstances.

There is one situation where fly fishers have a definite advantage over spin fishers. If a fish misses a lure or bait, spin fishers must reel in all the way in order to cast and present again. Fly fishers do not need to reel in order to cast again. They can simply execute a "pick-up-and-drop," which is just a back cast and forward cast that presents the fly again within the same area. This can be completed in a couple of seconds, hopefully before the fish heads elsewhere or loses its appetite.

Of course, effectiveness is a big concern. This is fishing and our primary goal is to catch fish. But this is also sport fishing and there are aspects of concern other than effectiveness. Fight is one of these areas and it's here that fly fishing rules. Due to the intrinsically light nature of the tackle, fighting a fish on a fly rod is a more intense experience than with conventional, spinning or even ultra-light spinning tackle. A long, light fly rod is ultrasensitive and becomes electrified when playing a fish.

The traditional procedure for handling small to medium-size fish on a fly rod is to strip the line in by hand rather than cranking the line in on the reel. When describing this to someone who has never experienced it, the only analogy I can make is that it feels like pulling on a Venetian blind with something pulling back at you.

Larger fish are played directly from the reel because it's smoother, and if the fish decides to run, the drag feature of the reel creates resistance and slows down and tires the fish.

Some experts today recommend playing the fish from the reel regardless of the size of the fish because it is smoother, but I still enjoy stripping the fish in. There's something so direct about feeling the fish through the line, giving ground when the fish fights hard and taking in the right amount of line at the right time.

Often I wind up using a combination of these techniques, stripping at first and then reeling in the slack. Whether you choose one or a combination of both methods, nothing beats battling a fish on a fly rod.

Compactness and portability are two side benefits of fly fishing. Other than rod and reel, all other tackle involved in fly fishing is small and light. Everything you need fits easily into the pockets of a light fishing vest. What a blessing it is not to have to lug a tackle box or bag around with you. Although it's possible to travel light while practicing other types of fishing, fly fishing lends itself to this naturally because you don't need heavy weights, large lures or bait containers. What a pleasure not to worry about getting bait, keeping it alive, keeping your hands reasonably clean, and keeping other members of your household from having a fit when they find strange things crawling around in the refrigerator.

I'm not a snob when it comes to fishing. I believe you can study and practice any type of fishing and never learn all there is to learn. It's a question of how deep you want to go. The depth of any subject is the dimension that's determined by personal choice. The breadth of a subject is intrinsic. Fly fishing, especially for trout, is a very broad subject.

Since the larger portion of a trout's diet consists of aquatic insects, fishing for them opens up a whole other vast and fascinating subject: entomology. The life cycle of these aquatic insects has a tremendous effect on the feeding of, and fishing for, trout.

Volumes have been written and lifetimes devoted to the study of aquatic entomology. That's not to say that you have to be an entomologist to catch trout on a fly rod, but there's plenty to learn if you choose to.

Fly tying adds a whole other dimension to the sport. There are thousands of traditional patterns which you can learn to tie. These patterns can be altered and adjusted to work in different situations and you can design completely new patterns of your own if you desire. Again, the level of involvement depends on how deep you wish to go. Catching a fish on a fly that you've tied yourself is something to be proud of and is highly rewarding.

Even if you never tie a fly yourself, tying small flies onto a thin tippet will have a positive effect on your rigging skills. It'll also make you crazy on occasion.

Although fly fishing may include topics that you can study for a lifetime, it can also be practiced and enjoyed easily by a beginner who is not wealthy, a genius, or an athlete.

Once you start fly fishing, I'm sure you'll come up with some of your own answers to: "Why fly fish?" and your only remaining question will be: "Why didn't I get into this sooner?"

Rainbow Trout

Rods

The purpose of a fly rod is two-fold: casting and fish fighting. Fly rods are described in terms of their length and their capacity to handle a certain weight line. Lines normally run from number 1 weight as the lightest to number 12 weight as the heaviest. When describing a rod, you'd say for instance: "It was an 8 ½' for 5 weight line" or "a 6' for a 3 weight line," etc. Sometimes weights fall between the numbers and are expressed as 3/4 or 5/6. This means the rod is capable of casting either line comfortably.

Most rods are made from either graphite, fiberglass or bamboo. Other materials and combinations of materials have been tried but these three have been the most popular. Graphite is the most modern of these materials and therefore the most commonly used. Fiberglass preceded graphite. It is less popular as a material for today's fly rods, but still possesses qualities which are desirable for certain types of rods, and seems to be experiencing a renaissance. Bamboo, or split cane, was the material of choice before fiberglass. It is a lovely fly rod material with a great tradition. It requires highly skilled craftsmanship to make rods from this material.

Reel Seat

Starting at the butt end of the rod, we have the reel seat which is mounted over the blank. It holds the reel in place and can be either a screw thread or sliding ring device. (Some older rods have a spring loaded seat.) Screw locking seats can be up or down-locking. Heavier rods are more often down-locking, lighter rods often up-locking. (This is simply a choice of the manufacturer and has no bearing on how well the reel is held in place.) Very light rods often feature two sliding rings which move freely on the seat and hold the reel in place by sliding over the reel foot.

> *Some larger rods have a "fighting butt." This is an extension situated below the reel seat. They range in length from anywhere between about 1 to 4 inches. Their purpose is to create more leverage and stability when fighting larger fish. They can be used for a two-handed grip or braced against the body.*

Fighting Butt

The rod handle is situated immediately in front of the seat. Handles are also mounted over the blank. They're most often made of cork or occasionally foam. On rare occasion they're made of wood. They come in various shapes and styles. Choosing one is a matter of the size and shape of your hands and generally how it feels to you.

Fly Rod Handles

Cigar

Half Wells

Reverse Half Wells

Full Wells

Following the handle are the guides, which are wound onto the blank with thread and sealed with varnish or epoxy. First we have the hook keeper which is not truly a guide but a small wire loop for holding the hook of a fly when the rod is rigged up but not in use. (Not all rods have hook keepers.) Next is the stripping guide. It is a closed-circle spinning-type guide. It is the first guide the line goes through when leaving the reel, and the last the line comes through when stripped or reeled back in.

Hook Keeper

Stripping Guide

A series of snake guides which diminish in size are spaced proportionally along the rest of the blank. They're thin wire, S-shaped loops which enable the fly line to travel through them with ease. At the tip of the rod, we have the tip top, a simple circular or pear-shaped loop of thin wire.

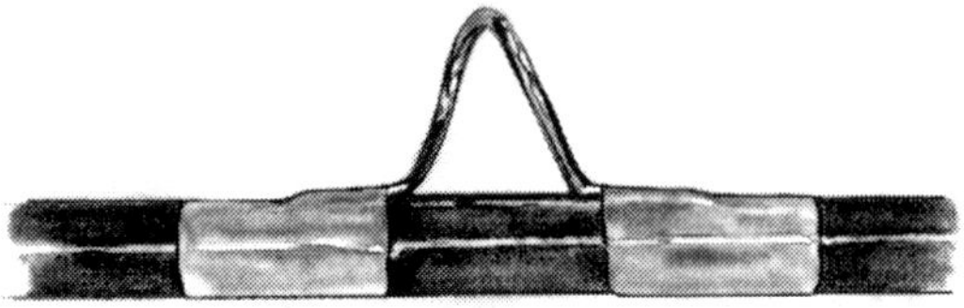

Snake Guide

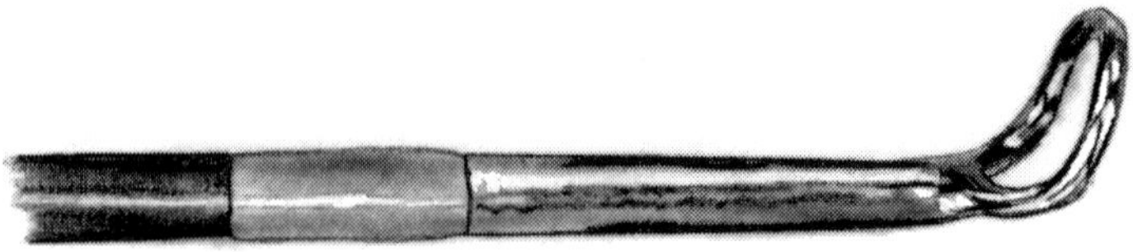

Tip Top

Since fly rods tend to be lengthy, they are usually divided into sections for the sake of portability. They are available in many different configurations, generally from two to seven piece sections. These sections are joined with ferrules, devices that enable a strong and easy connection between them. On bamboo rods, the ferrules are made of metal and glued to the blank. Older fiberglass rods may also have metal ferrules. Newer fiberglass and graphite rods have ferrules made from the same material as the blank.

Ferrule

In the past, ferrules lessened a rod's casting ability because they created stiff spots in the blank which interfered with its flexibility. This factor weighed against choosing a multi-section rod. Today's ferrules are so well designed that the number of sections hardly has any effect on the rod's casting ability. Portability has become an important consideration due to the increase of travel. A four-piece rod breaks down to a size that easily fits into an airplane overhead compartment, not to mention a car trunk.

The action of a rod is described in terms of slow, medium or fast. This simply refers to the amount of the rod which flexes when it's working. A fast rod flexes at the tip of the blank only. A medium rod flexes further down the blank and a slow action rod flexes throughout the blank down to the butt.

In general, faster rods are better for distance casting, but require precise timing as to when to begin the forward cast, and are not great tools for accurate and delicate presentations.

Progressive, or slower action rods, generally don't cast as far, but are more forgiving to cast and better tools for accurate and delicate presentation.

Rod Actions

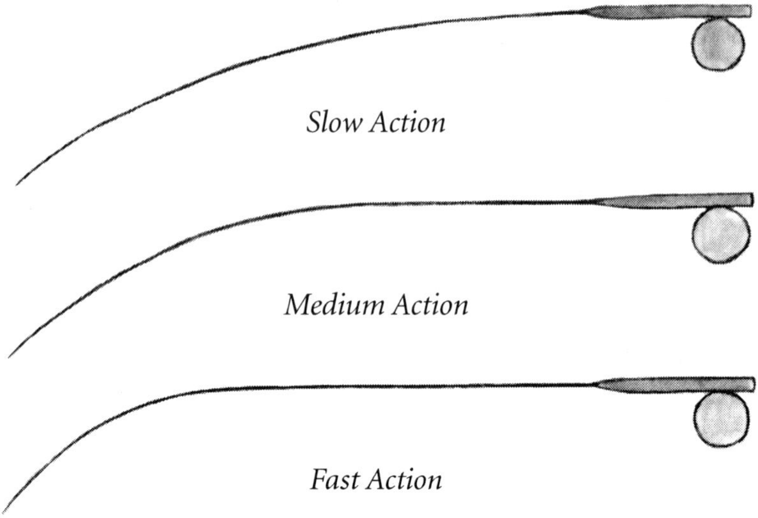

Reels

There are three major types of reels: single action, multipliers, and automatics. Single action reels are simple mechanisms that create one turn of the spool for each turn of the handle. A single-action reel is preferred for most fishing, especially trout fishing.

Multipliers are reels which are designed with a gear ratio which enables them to create more than one turn of the spool for each turn of the handle. They're designed for situations where it's necessary to retrieve a lot of line quickly. They're used mainly for saltwater, particularly for bonefish, which have a tendency to run and take large amounts of line off the reel.

Automatic reels incorporate a spring mechanism which is wound as line is stripped off the reel. The line is then retrieved automatically when the spring is activated.

Originally marketed as a labor saving device, an automatic is a bit of an unnecessary gimmick for most people and is hardly ever seen today. However, these reels are invaluable to someone with a disability who is not able to operate a regular reel. For this purpose they are a godsend and they enable a great number of people to fly fish who otherwise would not be able to.

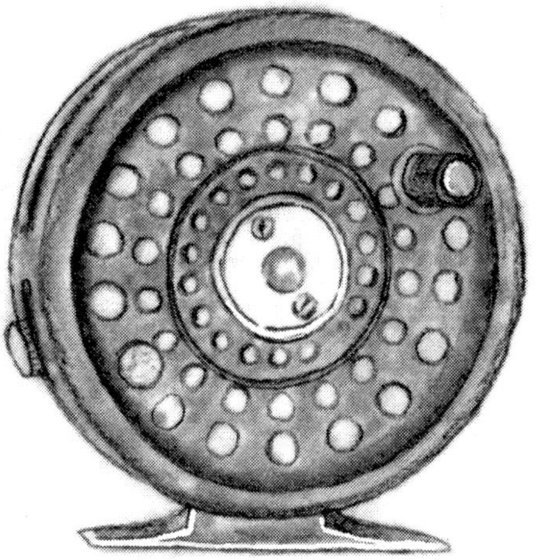

Fly Reel

Drags

On a fly reel, a drag system is used to create resistance on line coming off the reel, thereby tiring the fish and taking direct pressure off the leader so it will not break.

There are several types of drag systems used in fly reels. The two most common are click-and-pawl and disc drags. Click-and-pawl systems consist of a pawl or tongue of steel attached to a piece of spring steel for tension and racheted into a gear. Adjusting the tension of the spring increases or decreases the amount of drag. Often the system includes two pawls so that the reel is adjustable for either right-handed or left-handed retrieval.

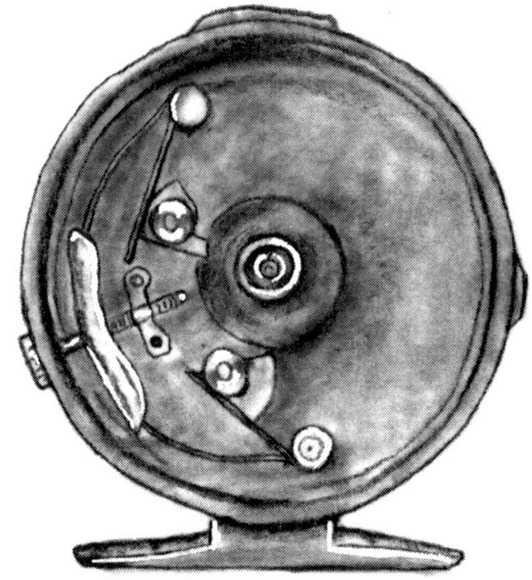

Click-And-Pawl

Although an older design, click-and-pawl drags are effective for most fishing where the fish are small or medium in size.

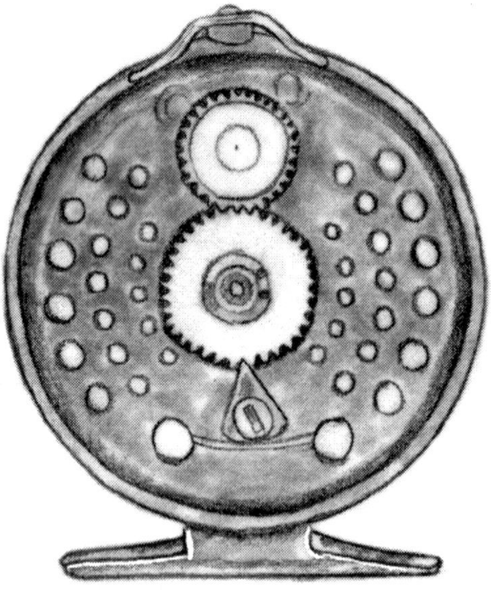

Disc Drag

Disc drag systems consist of a disk of thin material such as cork or Teflon® which acts as a pressure plate creating more or less friction to increase or decrease the drag. Disc drags are more effective than click-and-pawl drags. When they were first introduced they were more expensive than click-and-pawl drags but are now equally affordable. For saltwater or any situation where you may hook into large fish, a disc drag is preferred.

There are other types of drag systems but today most reels have either disc or click-and-pawl drags.

Lines

Since the weight of the fly is usually inconsequential, the fly line provides the weight necessary to bend (load) the rod so it's able to cast.

Lines are classified by three designations: weight, taper and function. They're coded using letters and numbers to represent these. For example, a WF-5-F means a weight forward taper, 5 weight, floating line. A DT-8-S would indicate a double taper, 8 weight, sinking line, etc. The taper of a fly line is its basic design and determines its casting properties.

A weight forward line has a heavy, thicker tapered section in the first quarter of the line and then a thinner, lighter section for the remainder of the line. The theory of this design is based on the heavy front section's ability to load (bend) the rod quickly.

A double taper line has tapered sections at both ends of the line (only one of these is in use at a time) and a level running (mid) section between these. The theory here is that the consistent diameter of the running section creates more stability, thus allowing for more delicate presentations.

Its more even weight distribution allows the line to be lifted off the water more easily and delicately and enables you to roll cast more easily.

A level line has no taper and isn't used for casting flies. It's used for trolling and bait fishing (yes, people did and still do baitfish with a fly rod) where the weight needed to cast is provided by the bait.

Line Tapers

Weight Forward

Double Taper

These are the three major taper designs. In addition, there are many other tapers which are all subtle variations of these.

The weight of a fly line is determined by its physical weight and thickness. The weight of the line doesn't have a direct correlation to its ability to hold a fish. (A fly line is a heavy, strong line. Even a 1-weight line wouldn't break against a tremendous fish.) But since the line must be used in coordination with a suitable rod and the strength of the rod determines what weight fish it will hold, the two are indirectly correlated.

The function of a fly line is determined by its buoyancy. Floating lines are completely buoyant and stay on the surface of the water. Sinking lines descend into the water at various rates of speed for fishing at different depths and are designated accordingly.

> *Since the average length of a fly line is about 90' it will not fill the entire reel. In order to accommodate this we use "backing." "Backing" is braided Dacron® line from 20 to 30 lb. test. It is tied and spooled onto the empty reel in the necessary amount and attached to the fly line.*

Backing will also serve to extend the length of the line in situations where fish make long runs, pulling large amounts of line off the reel. This may happen with very large fish or certain species such as bonefish that have an innate tendency to do this.

Leaders

Because of the large diameter of a fly line, it is necessary to attach a length of thinner material to the line in order to make it possible to tie on a fly. This length of line (usually monofilament) is the leader. Leaders come in various lengths and tippet sizes. In most cases, they are designed to taper from a larger diameter at its butt section which attaches to the fly line, to a smaller diameter at the end which will be tied to the fly. This section of thin diameter leader is called the tippet section. It usually runs about 24" at that same thin diameter.

Leaders come in one piece that is already tapered or in several lengths of diminishing size pieces of line which have been knotted together to form a taper.

Some fly fisherman tie their own knotted leaders in order to create a specific, customized-designed leader, and also to save money.

Tippet

As you change flies you clip off small pieces of the tippet section of your leader. Since your leader is tapered it will eventually become too short and its diameter too thick. Instead of replacing the entire leader (which would become very costly), you can replace the tippet section by tying a new piece on to the remaining leader.

Tippet material comes in small spools so it can easily be stored and carried in your vest. It comes in various sizes to accommodate different fishing situations. You may change tippets and even entire leaders several times a day according to need.

Tippet size is designated by a number followed by an x. The larger the number, the smaller the tippet size and vice versa. Thus a 7x tippet is very light and would be about 1.5 pound test and a 2x tippet would be about 5 pound test.

Choice of tippet size is determined by three factors: the size of the fly, the size of fish you are catching or expect to catch, and the clarity of the water you are fishing in. Clearer waters render heavier tippets more visible when they are presented, and therefore call for a lighter tippet. Tippets of a small diameter such as 7x or 6x would normally be used for small dry flies and nymphs, 5x and 4x for larger flies such as wet flies or small streamers, and 3x and heavier for bass and saltwater flies.

Salmon

WHERE TO FISH

Most fly fishermen consider fishing for trout on moving water the high end of fly fishing. If you're fortunate enough to live near a good trout stream or river, or have the means to travel to one, great, go fishing and enjoy. If you don't, don't worry. There are options.

I don't know the exact figures, but most people in the U.S. live near a body of warm water (lakes and ponds) and these usually contain panfish and bass.

I live in Queens, the largest of New York City's five boroughs. There are three ponds within ten minutes of my house. Each of these has large populations of largemouth bass, carp, sunfish, crappies and catfish. One of these ponds is situated a short block off a main road, behind a large apartment building. It's a pretty pond surrounded by a well-wooded area, which provides a home to an abundant variety of animal and bird life, yet its location has rendered it unknown to much of the local population.

Somehow because of its urban setting, people refuse to believe it contains fish, especially big fish. Yet I have taken sizeable bass up to four pounds, a carp of ten pounds and had great sport with a variety of panfish in a pond located within the limits of one of the largest cities in the world.

Largemouth bass can be found in urban and suburban lakes and ponds, farm ponds, sumps and other unlikely places. Usually wherever you find bass you'll find their smaller cousins, the sunfishes. "Sunnies" come in many varieties: bluegills, pumpkinseeds, red ears and others. They all have one thing in common: they're fast, fierce and feisty. Pound per pound, they're better fighters than bass and much faster.

Although they are very catchable and will often accept almost any fly you throw at them, there are times when sunfish won't touch anything, thereby adding enough challenge to keep the game interesting.

A sunfish will often inhale a fly and spit it back out again in a heartbeat. This creates an ideal situation for practicing hook-setting. All these qualities make sunfish the perfect target for the novice fly fisher. Nevertheless some very experienced fly rodders prefer to fish for them. I know two veteran fly fishermen who fish for them almost exclusively, using all their fishing and casting expertise to score when other anglers can't get a nibble.

Sometimes while you are retrieving a sunfish, a largemouth bass will attack it because the sunnie is stressed and swimming erratically and is now easy prey. A very patient fly fisherman can often land a largemouth engorged on a sunnie. When this happens you soon realize that the amount of time you spend retrieving the sunnie is the thin line between fly fishing and live-lining sunfish. This situation is a temptation that tests the temper of your sportsmanship. This is a good thing though, because as well as knowledge and skills, sportsmanship is best learned though experience.

Although I've yet to do it, carp can also be taken on a fly. I've caught them on spinning tackle and I can only imagine what a blast it must be to hook into one of these monsters on a fly rod. This once-maligned fish was for many years considered a "garbage fish." Today, it's finally being recognized as a fine game fish. It has all the qualities of bonefish; being spooky and requiring a delicate presentation, and running great lengths of line in a short time, and as a plus, they fight harder. It's about time they received the credit they deserve. If you choose to fish for them, you probably won't have much trouble finding them. Carp are survivors and can be found in all kinds of water from still, murky ponds to fast, clear streams and anything in between.

If you live on either coast, you have the world of saltwater fly fishing available to you. Saltwater fly rodding has been exploding in popularity in the past few years. The size of the fish alone is enough to get you involved. Striped bass, bluefish, bonita, sea trout, redfish, bonefish, tarpon and many others readily take a fly. The battles these fish give are highly intensified on a fly rod.

> *Since larger rods and anti-corrosive reels are generally in order for saltwater, equipment is usually more expensive, but there are ways to outfit yourself at a reasonable cost.*

So unless you live in a desert, there's no excuse to sit around and dream of that trip to New Zealand while your waders dry-rot. Get out there and fish. The old saw is true: "You can't catch fish with your line out of the water."

Chain Pickerel

Rods

The length and line weight of your rod is basically determined by the type of fishing you'll be doing with it. Rods between 7½' and 8½' long are used for most fishing situations.

Since they generally cast further, longer rods of 9' to 10' are intended for fishing bigger waters such as large rivers, large lakes and saltwater. Long rods are also preferable for fishing from canoes, kayaks and float tubes, because in these situations you're positioned lower and closer to the water and need the height of the rod to be able to lift the line off the water when casting or trying to hook or land a fish.

Short rods 6' to 7' can be helpful when fishing tiny creeks and streams which are brushy and overgrown.

All of the above are normal fly rod lengths. There are rods both longer and shorter than these, but they are too specialized to be of concern to the beginner.

The line weight of your outfit is determined by two factors: the size of the flies you wish to cast and the size of the fish you're targeting.

When you're first starting out, these questions may be difficult to answer. An 8'-5 or 6 weight outfit is a good bet for something that best serves a number of different fishing situations. Increments of 6 inches in length or 1 weight up or down are subtleties, so if you come across something that's slightly different from an ideal 8'-5 weight, it's okay.

If you're going to be fishing mostly for small trout or pan fish, a 4 weight rod is a good choice. For sizable largemouth bass, a 7 weight is appropriate. For salmon, steelhead and most saltwater species, I recommend an 8 or 9 weight.

Again, these are just rough guidelines – not hard and fast rules.

Rods for 3, 2 and 1 weight lines have recently become very popular. It's just my personal opinion, but I feel anything below a 4 weight is silly. A small trout or even a small sunfish will give you quite a nice fight on a 4 weight. Anything less than that just seems to become harder to cast. But that's just my opinion. A lot of this depends on personal preference. First and foremost the rod should feel right for you.

The action of the rod is probably the factor that most affects individual preference. A slower action rod enables you to feel the cast and is generally more forgiving and usually a good choice for a beginner. I personally prefer slower or at least medium action rods for most fishing, especially for trout fishing where distance casting isn't always needed. The trend in today's rods is to make them stiffer or faster. So finding a slower or medium action rod requires a little more effort, but in my opinion, is well worth it. Faster action rods are preferable for fishing big water, especially saltwater. Again, a stiffer rod requires a more precise sense of timing while casting, and this can be tricky for a beginner.

Whenever possible, try to cast a rod before you buy it. Most fly fishing shops have an area where you can try out a rod. If you can't try it out, make sure you can return it if you don't like it. No matter what it costs or what the manufacturer claims or what someone else says, the rod must feel right to you. The only true test is casting the rod. Even casting it on land doesn't give you a complete picture of how the rod will perform. Factors like how the rod roll casts (which will be described later in the book) can only be tested on the water, and its fish-fighting abilities obviously can't be measured until you've caught fish with it, so a good return policy is still in order even if you've cast it at the store.

Obviously you'll want a rod that's made with quality materials and components. That's not much of a problem because regardless of what the manufacturer's ads say, most rod blanks are much the same, and even inexpensive fly rods are usually made with decent components. If anything, the components used on more expensive rods are overkill. For instance, most guides are made of steel and are chrome-plated. They are quite durable and will probably last longer than you or me, yet there are rods that feature titanium/nitrate guides or tungsten/carbide guides which are much more durable than chrome-plated steel. Considering the advances in the slickness of fly line coatings, it's unlikely you'll wear through the guides of a fly rod even during a lifetime of fishing, so in most cases this is overkill. I guess some manufacturers feel they must do something to justify their prices.

The high prices of some fly rods are totally inexcusable. Spinning rods have more handle area and the guides are more expensive, yet you can purchase a great spinning rod for a reasonable cost. Fly rod manufacturers will often tell you that since the market for spinning gear is so much larger, spin gear manufacturers can mark down their product to a low price and still make a profit. This may be true to a degree, but not enough to justify the difference in cost between the two items.

High priced fly rods often come with lifetime guarantees, but that still doesn't seem to justify their price. The main reason for these inflated prices is that the market will bear it. Somehow a yuppie attitude of "It must be better because it costs more" has taken hold. Don't despair. You can purchase a good fly rod for a decent price.

Quite often the same shops that sell rods which require you to take out a second mortgage on your house will also carry rods and reels or sets which include rods, reels, line and backing for a very good price.

Catalogs often feature a number of reasonably-priced rods or sets and although you can't try these out, they usually have liberal return polices.

Large chain sporting goods stores usually have a nice selection of low-priced but good equipment.

Fly fishing and sportsmen's shows are a great place for bargains. Dealers and manufacturers have paid for space at these shows and are willing to sell low in order to move products, cover the cost of the show and to increase their visibility. Shows almost always have casting platforms where you can try out the rod.

Used equipment is another possibility. A lot of people didn't have the opportunity to read this book and therefore became frustrated and gave up the sport early on. They're often willing to sell equipment at a fraction of its original cost. Ads for used equipment can be found in local buy-and-sell newspapers, club newsletters, posted on bulletin boards and on the Internet.

There are often great bargains on the Internet, especially on auction sites. But a word of caution here: it's easy to get caught up in a bidding war and wind up paying more than the item is worth. With old or second-hand equipment, the value of the item may be somewhat subjective, so ask around about what something is worth before placing that bid. With new equipment, you should do some research to try to determine the approximate retail cost. I've see new rods sell for a much higher price than you'd pay at a retail store simply because the bidders got carried away with the game. New or used, try to have some frame of reference for the item's price.

Beginners who hope to fish for trout, pan fish or even bass should consider a fiberglass rod. Fiberglass was overshadowed by graphite when it first appeared on the market and was touted as the new space age material. Graphite is lighter than fiberglass and usually stiffer. Fiberglass still makes a fine fly rod and in most cases is incredibly less expensive. There are some tasks where fiberglass outperforms graphite and vice versa. Since fiberglass is a softer material than graphite, it usually makes a slower rod. As I mentioned before, this quality creates a more forgiving casting tool, which is a plus for the novice fly fisher. Still, many experienced fly fishers prefer fiberglass, especially for trout fishing on smaller waters.

It's strange that although bamboo and fiberglass are materials with similar qualities in regard to the speed of the blank and its casting abilities, bamboo is usually applauded for this, whereas fiberglass is often denigrated for these same qualities. Why? Probably because bamboo has something fiberglass doesn't: snob appeal.

Although it may seem a tall order for your first rod, building a rod might be a consideration down the road. It not only can save you a lot of money, but it can be customized to your exact specifications. If you're handy, it's not a tremendously difficult task. The experience of catching a fish on a rod you've built yourself will add another dimension to the sport.

> *I have a friend who's a very experienced fly fisherman. I consider him the best fisherman I know. He has fished all over the world. He is a member of the prestigious "Angler's Club" of Manhattan. He owns all kinds of rods. We were on a trip and stopped at a major discount sporting goods chain to pick up some leaders. I pointed out a very inexpensive fiberglass rod that I admired. He liked it and bought it. Since then, he has hardly fished with anything else. He loved it so much that he went out and bought about six of them as presents for his friends.*
>
> *I'm telling this story to emphasize my point about a rod being a good rod if it works for you. Don't be swayed by price or hype.*

Reels

For many years the opinion of most experts was that a fly reel's principal purpose was to store line. For the most part, that still holds true. In fishing for small to medium size fish, you usually strip in the line and reel it up afterwards. Traditionally, the reel was not used directly. Lately, it has been more fashionable to play the fish with the reel. Some claim this is important because the action of the reel is much smoother than stripping. I agree, but only when it comes to fighting larger fish.

Larger fish will often run and it's here where a reel becomes handy. (A running fish must be left to run in order to tire it out.)

The drag feature of the reel is the device that creates resistance when the line is being stripped from the reel. When fishing for certain species that tend to run (like bonefish), drag is a handy feature. Additional drag can also be created by palming the spool of the reel to create resistance and thereby slowing down the running line. Palming can only be done on a reel with an exposed rim. An exposed rim is simply one where the rim of the spool is not enclosed by a cage (a round frame or casing.) Most modern reels have exposed rims. Only some older models are the caged type.

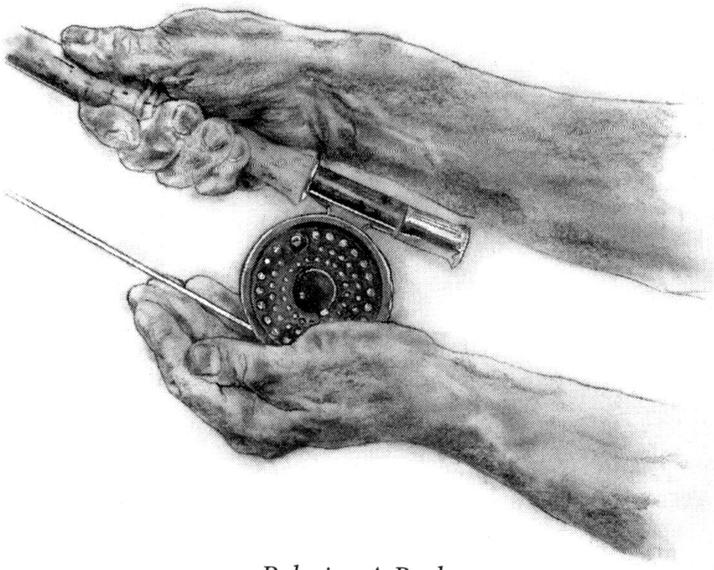

Palming A Reel

Whether or not to fight small or medium size fish directly from the reel is one of those fly fishing arguments that will go on forever. My stance here is: do whatever you're comfortable with, whatever works for you. As I mentioned earlier, I use a combination of the stripping and reeling methods, depending on how I feel at the time.

I'm explaining all of this because it does affect your choice of reels. If you're going to be fishing for large fish that run, you'll probably need a reel with a strong drag system such as a disc drag.

For saltwater fishing, a reel that's anti-corrosive is also a good bet, but if you can't afford a reel with either of these features, you can still fish saltwater with a reel that has an exposed rim for palming. If it isn't anti-corrosive, you just have to be careful to keep it well lubricated and make sure you rinse it well after each use.

For normal trout and largemouth bass fishing, a simple single action click-and-pawl reel does just fine. Again, reels of this type are very affordable. You can also find disc drag reels at reasonable prices. Yes, more expensive reels are often better made. Some are really finely crafted little machines. But are they necessary? No. Will you catch more or larger fish by using them? No.

Lines

Most beginner's instructions recommend starting out with a weight forward line. Weight forward lines load the rod easily and are reputedly better than double taper lines for distance casting. Traditionally, double taper lines are considered better for delicate presentations and for roll-casting. Double tapers are also easier to lift off the water than weight forwards, because not all of the weight is up front. The logic for starting out with a weight forward line was most likely based on the fact that in the past, double tapers were probably more difficult to cast. I don't think this is the case anymore. Although the designs are basically the same as they were, fly line materials have improved so greatly in the last few years, that I personally don't find double tapers any more difficult to cast than weight forwards. To me, the advantages of delicate presentation, easier lift-off and roll casting ability outweigh the slight distance advantage of weight forward lines.

The other very important consideration is cost. Every couple of seasons you will find that your fly line has had it and needs to be replaced. Fly lines are not cheap. A double taper line is really two lines in one. When it's worn out, you simply turn it around and use the end that was wound on the reel. So in essence, a double taper line is half the cost of a weight forward. That alone is enough to convince me.

Leaders

For trout and panfish, a couple of 9 foot, 5x tapered leaders will be fine to start off with. If you need anything with a smaller tippet size, you can always add a piece of tippet material. Longer leaders are better for more delicate presentations, when fishing for spooky fish in clear shallow water or for fishing very small flies.

Some instructors advocate tying a piece of same size tippet onto a tapered leader. I have never understood the logic here since the manufacturers go to great pains to design these leaders, and any additional tippet material of the same size will make it more difficult for the leader to turn over the fly during the cast.

Some advanced fly fishermen make their own custom leaders by tying together pieces of monofilament in diminishing diameters to create a tapering effect. They do this for two purposes: to create a special leader for a specific type of fishing and to save money. For some reason leaders made this way are for sale over-the-counter. I have never understood this since it serves neither of the above-mentioned purposes.

Tippet

Remember, every time you change flies, you will be cutting off a piece of the tippet section of your leader. At a certain point, the leader will be too thick and short and you will then need to add tippet material.

Tippet material comes rolled onto small spools so that it can be easily carried in your vest. Tippets are designated by x size; the larger the number the smaller the diameter of the tippet.

A spool of 4x, 5x and 6x tippet will cover most of your needs. If you find yourself fishing for very spooky fish or in very clear, shallow water or for fish feeding on very small flies, you may need to use 7x. If you are fishing for large bass, 3x or even 2x may be necessary.

For saltwater, I prefer fluorocarbon tippet material. This stuff can be costly if you buy the small rolls. Instead, I buy large rolls of fluorocarbon line sold for spin fishing. It comes to about one-fourth of the cost. I then roll it on empty tippet spools. For most saltwater fishing, 10 to 20 pound test tippet will cover you.

Vests

A fishing vest is basically a tackle box that you wear. It hardly provides any protection from the cold, although it creates enough warmth to cause some discomfort when the weather is extremely hot.

Obviously, a vest must have enough pockets to hold all of your equipment. This is a difficult thing to determine when you're first starting out.

Bear in mind that you'll probably increase the amount of stuff you carry within your first couple of years of fly fishing and then you'll most likely start to pare it down when you realize that you never use some of the stuff you've been carrying around for years.

The largest items you'll be carrying in your vest will be your fly boxes. I carry a minimum of four and a maximum of six. Most vests will accommodate that many.

The number of fly boxes you carry depends on what you're fishing for and how you box up your flies. You'll be continually changing your system as your needs change.

Tippet is probably the next largest item, and although even several spools don't consume that much space, you'll want to be sure the vest you choose has enough tippet pockets and that they are easily accessible.

The space consumed by the other gadgets and sundries you may need or want is of little consequence, but a number of little pockets on both the outside and inside of a vest can be handy.

The fleece patches you see on some vests are supposed to be for drying flies. Instead they seem to serve as a great place to put your flies if you want to be sure to lose them.

Ripple foam patches that pin on to your vest are much better and it seems that there are new ones made of different materials or that work on some new principle or design being introduced every so often. I haven't tried any other than the ripple foam, so you're on your own there. Just remember, these patches are primarily for the purpose of drying flies which you're not using at the time. Try to get into the habit of putting other flies back into their boxes after they're well dried.

Another thing to look for in a vest is a knitted collar. A loaded vest can become heavy enough to create pressure and discomfort around your neck. Also, remember that the vest you try on in the store is empty. Don't be embarrassed to ask the sales person to put a couple of things in the pockets so you can tell how it will really feel when you're fishing. Your vest should also have a ring on the back where you can hang a net.

If most of your fishing will be done during hot weather, you may want a vest with a mesh back or one that's at least made of 100% cotton. For fishing year round I would suggest one made of a cotton polyester mixture.

As you become more experienced, you may find yourself carrying less gear. You also may need less gear because of specific fishing situations such as saltwater fishing which generally requires fewer flies or any situation where you feel comfortable carrying less.

At this point you may want to look at alternatives to the vest. There are many. A chest pack may be a good choice. They come in various sizes and configurations to suit different needs. They usually have a strap which goes around your neck, and sometimes another which straps around the waist for stabilization. Some are combined with small backpacks as well. Others are kind of pack/vest hybrids. There seems to be a new alternative every season.

Often a fishing shirt with multiple pockets will accommodate all the gear you need. Many prefer neck lanyards for hanging tools such as nippers and hemostats. The light fishing shirt and neck lanyard have become the popular choice for flats fishing in the

> *tropics where heat is a concern.*
>
> *There are really no rules here. Carry your gear in whatever fashion you find most comfortable.*

Waders

If you're on a budget or just want to first feel out what kind of fishing you'll be doing, you can fish without waders and still do quite well. A lot of stillwater fishing can be done successfully right from the shore. It is often a better strategy to fish some streams without wading in them at all, stalking cautiously up to the bank and keeping a low profile so you don't spook the fish.

Still, it's nice to have the ability to wade, and in some cases, it will make the difference between being able to fish or not.

The many different styles of waders and the materials they're made from can be baffling to a beginner. First, let's deal with styles. Waders are either boot foot or stocking foot style. A boot foot wader has rubber boots permanently attached to the rest of the wader. A stocking foot wader ends with a sock-like foot like those on a pair of kids' pajamas. These require a separate pair of wading shoes.

Each of these has advantages and disadvantages. Boot foot waders are easier to put on. You simply slip on the waders and you're ready, whereas stocking foot waders require you to put on the waders first and then a separate pair of wading shoes. Stocking foot waders are more comfortable. Boot foot tend to feel somewhat clunky.

It's less costly to buy a pair of boot foot waders than a pair of stocking foot plus separate wading shoes. On the other hand, you may have a couple of different pairs of stocking foot waders that you can use with the same wading shoes, so at least there is some savings there. Comfort seems to be the major difference, so if you can afford it, I would recommend the stocking foot waders and separate wading shoes. The only exception I can think of is that boot foot waders are better for wading in places with muddy bottoms such as some saltwater bays. Often this is the case simply because it's easier to clean a smooth one-piece rubber boot than a lace-up shoe.

Waders come in various heights; chest-high, waist-high and hip boots (also called hippers.) Your choice of course depends on the depth of the water you'll be wading. As you get more involved, you may want a couple of pairs for different situations.

> *For guys, there's always the issue of fly-access (I don't mean the ones you fish with.) I've always said that the person who invents a pair of waders with a fly will make a fortune. Until then, hippers have the distinct advantage of easy fly access over chest or waist-high waders. I'll opt for hippers whenever I can get away with it. Aside from that, they are generally more comfortable because there is less of them.*

Waders are constructed from various materials. Nylon/rubber or PVC-coated are some of the least expensive waders on the market. At one time, waders made from these materials were the only type available. They were and are heavy, clunky and uncomfortable. Even if you're on a tight budget, forget about these.

Nylon waders come in various weights. There are extremely heavy models for duck hunters. They need the durability of this material for its ability to withstand the conditions they deal with in the places where they hunt. They aren't that concerned about comfort when moving about because they spend most of their time sitting still.

These heavy waders are definitely not for fly fishermen. Mid-weight nylons are better. They are still not the world's most comfortable. Because of their durability, I find them great for stream restoration work where waders receive a lot of punishment.

Lightweight nylon is better yet, but still not great because it doesn't breathe and therefore can cause you to work up quite a sweat.

Neoprene waders are still a good idea for extreme cold weather fishing. Aside from this, I can't think of any other advantage to them. They tend to leak easily and are form fitting, which not only makes them a pain to get on and off, but tends to exaggerate your form. (I'll let you decide whether you think this is a good or bad quality.)

Breathable waders are definitely the choice for today's fly fishers. In their earlier stages of development, they had a tendency to leak and were quite pricey. Nowadays, they have perfected the material and made them much more affordable.

Despite all of today's technological advances, much of fly fishing has remained the same for many years. In my opinion, the two areas most positively affected by improvements in technology have been fly line materials and wader materials. Breathable waders are a godsend. They are light as a feather, as comfortable as khakis and reasonably durable. You can wear them through the hottest summer weather and never break a sweat. During the winter, they will serve you well with a good pair of expedition-weight long johns or wading pants underneath, for all but the most extreme cold situations.

All things considered, breathables are the best way to go. You may be tempted to purchase a pair of less expensive waders made of one of the previously mentioned materials. Hold out if you can and save up for the breathables. I'm sure you'll find it worthwhile in the long run.

> *Safety Tip*
>
> ***All waders should be worn with a belt.*** *This will keep the waders from filling with water if you fall in. Once a pair of waders fills up it becomes very difficult to swim or even stand up in shallow water. You may then become exhausted and in danger of drowning! This inexpensive item will safeguard against this and can make* ***the difference between life and death****.*

Wading Shoes

Aside from the obvious qualities such as fit, comfort and construction, the most important thing to consider in a wading shoe is the sole.

In many wading situations you will be walking on very slippery surfaces and need a shoe with a sole that will provide the maximum traction.

For many years felt was the material of choice for this. More recently however we've discovered that felt can harbor and transport aquatic invasive pests, vegetation and diseases.

These problems are an extremely serious threat to the resource. Some of these problems have already rendered some waters unfishable. We must do everything possible to keep these problems in check.

There are now many "sticky rubber" soled wading shoes on the market which are as good as and sometimes even better than, felt. A number of these also have studs embedded in them for even greater traction. One of these is definitely the best choice.

> ***Safety Tip***
>
> *When wading in areas where there is a slippery bottom, fast water or rough rocks, always use a wading staff. A staff will serve both to support you and to probe spots that you are about to wade into.*
>
> *Staffs are available in collapsible models which are very convenient but can be pricey. Any stout stick of a hard material will suffice as a wading staff. I made one from bamboo which is light, durable and nice-looking.*
>
> *It is a good idea to tether the staff to yourself in order to have both hands free when necessary and to keep it from floating away if you accidentally drop it.*

Wading Jackets

Wading jackets are simply short rain jackets. They're designed so you can wade deeply without them draping into the water and getting soaked. They're made from various materials. Light nylon has the advantage of lightness and portability but doesn't seem to protect you too well during long periods of hard rain. PVC-coated nylon protects well and is reasonably priced, but I personally don't like the feel of it. It's kind of rubbery and not the most comfortable stuff for clothing. Some are made from a heavier nylon and are highly waterproof but tend to create warmth, which is a blessing in winter and the opposite in summer. Breathable is of course the best, but the most costly.

So which way to go? Well, the main consideration here is: how often will you need it? Naturally, you can't predict how much fishing you'll be doing in the rain. But think about the weather where you live to help make your decision. How much of a fishing nut you are can also help to answer the question. I fish a lot in all kinds of weather. I manage to do okay with a light nylon jacket for the spring and a heavy one for the fall and cooler saltwater fishing. Guides, who are on the water a couple of hundred days out of the year, find that it pays for them to invest in a good breathable jacket. This is one of those cases where you'll have to make the call on your own. If you're really on a budget or just can't decide, you can get away with a regular rain jacket for a while. The bottom will get wet, but it's not that great a tragedy since you're either wearing chest waders which cover you in that area, or hippers, which don't, in which case a longer jacket would be appropriate anyway.

Nets

If you're going to release all your fish, you really don't need a net. You can simply grab hold of the hook, turn it point down, and the fish will usually come off the hook. If it doesn't, the use of a hemostat will get the job done.

If you have any intention of keeping fish or even holding them long enough to snap a picture or take a long look, then a net is necessary.

The main thing I look for in a net is lightness. Laminated wood frame nets are traditional for fly fishing. They are quite beautiful and they look great hung on a wall, but I find them too heavy. I prefer an aluminum net. The one I own was dirt cheap and is real ugly, but it's light as a feather, so when it's hanging from my back I can hardly feel it. The actual difference in weight between an aluminum and a wood net is probably not much, but when it's hanging from your back all day, that small increase in weight begins to feel like a ton.

When I first acquired this net, these inexpensive aluminum frame types only came with that hard nylon netting. The soft "catch and release" netting was only available on the wooden nets. Since then they started making light aluminum nets with the softer "catch and release" netting. It didn't really matter to me because any fish I netted were going into the pan anyway, but with the soft netting you have a bit of an option. (I still advocate only netting fish that you intend to keep.)

Net Releases

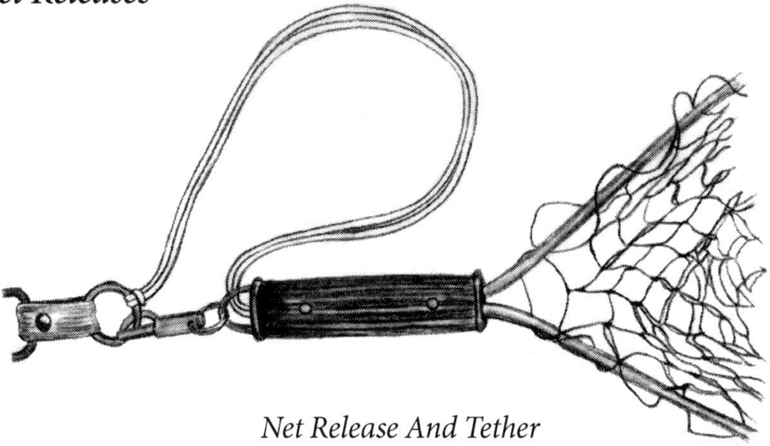

Net Release And Tether

A net release is a device which enables you to disconnect your net from the ring on the back of your vest or wading jacket, so you can use it and then reconnect it when you're finished with it. Hopefully, it'll work in a way which permits you to do this with ease.

There are many different types of these devices on the market. I find the best of these to be the magnetic type. A fairly strong magnet attaches the net to the ring. A slight tug frees the net. Reconnecting is simple. Just hold the net release in the neighborhood of its mate and let magnetism work its magic. A tether of some kind will prevent you from losing the net if it slips from your hand.

There are other devices that hold well and release easily enough but are tricky to reattach. I've seen large retractors used to hold nets in place. I don't like this system. When you access the net it is under pressure from the retractor. This restricts its use and if it slips out of your hand, it returns with a high velocity and can give you quite a wallop.

Fly Boxes

Boxes in which you can store your flies run the gamut from expensive monogrammed boxes made from exotic hardwoods that cost more than what I'd pay for a rod to breath mint tins which are included for free with the purchase of the mints. That choice depends on how important you consider a fly box as a fashion statement. How they are designed to hold your flies is a more practical consideration.

There are two basic designs of fly boxes: those that stow your flies in small compartments and those that hold your flies with some sort of clipping device or foam that secures the point of the fly hook. Both have their advantages and disadvantages.

Compartment type boxes are easy to use, requiring little if any maintenance. You simply put different flies in their own compartments. Unfortunately you could never have a box with enough compartments for each type of fly in each size. Even several boxes won't accommodate this need, so different sizes and sometimes even different patterns wind up sharing a compartment. This is not a major concern, but it means you'll have to dig a little to find the exact fly you want to use.

Boxes that are designed to either hold your flies with a clip or foam will enable you to see the exact fly you are searching for at a glance. The disadvantage here is that you'll have to take the time and effort it requires to keep each fly in its place. This is especially time consuming with foam boxes where each fly must be dug into the foam at the proper space from its neighbor as well as in some kind of logical order.

It all comes down to personality. Are you the type who is willing to invest the time and effort it takes to arrange flies in a meticulous order and are diligent enough to maintain them, or are you up for taking the time to search for the fly you need while the fish are rising at your feet? You don't need to strictly choose one or the other. You'll need several fly boxes so sometimes you can mix and match these designs to suit your flies as well as your needs and personality. These decisions and others will form your individual approach to the sport and help make it more personal.

Other Helpful Items

Nippers

A simple pair of line nippers are a necessity. The best ones look like nail clippers but are made from a single piece of spring steel. Some have a small needle on the end which is handy for clearing out hook eyes that have become clogged with head cement. Nippers are most easily accessed when they are attached to a retractor (also known as a "zinger.")

> **_Safety Tip_**
>
> *Using your teeth to cut monofilament line is a bad idea! The mono is stronger than the enamel on your teeth and biting it causes small chips in the enamel.*

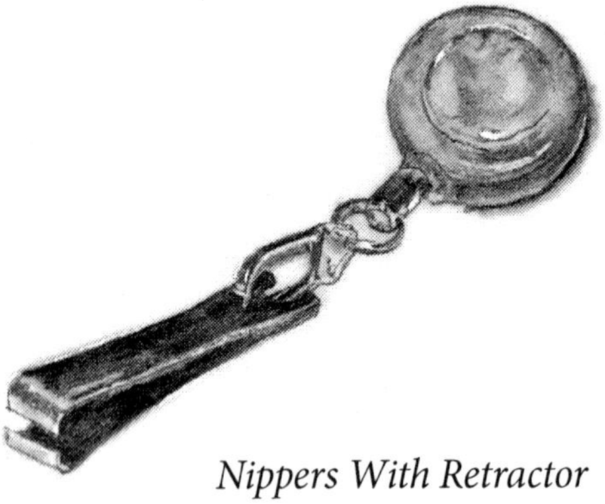

Nippers With Retractor

Hemostats

Hemostats are small surgical clamps with a scissor-like grip. They are great for removing hooks that are deeply embedded in fish. It's not necessary to attach them to a zinger. Just clip them to a convenient pocket flap or the edge of your vest.

Hemostats

Floatant

Floatant is applied to dry flies to help them float. It comes in many different forms: liquid, gel, crystals, sprays and probably others that I'm not familiar with. I like the gel type which comes in a small plastic squeeze bottle with an attached cap. It's easy to dispense and access. You squeeze a small amount out, rub it between your thumb and forefinger and then onto the fly. Floatant is a fairly inexpensive article, so try a couple and see which you prefer.

Pliers

A small pair of jeweler's pliers are a handy tool for smashing down barbs on hooks.

I prefer to either smash down the barbs or use barbless hooks for my flies. Obviously, a barbless hook does less damage to a fish and therefore is best to use when you intend to release your fish. Even if you intend to keep fish, a barbless hook will give you the option of creating less damage if the fish you hook is too small to keep. Although there is no irrevocable proof, it's highly possible that barbless hooks make for easier hook-ups because of their ability to penetrate more easily.

Safety Tip

Conversely, a barbless hook is easier to remove, so if you accidentially hook yourself – you can get it out without too much fuss. A barbed hook embedded in some part of your body will often require minor surgery to remove it!

Hook Sharpeners

Get into the habit of sharpening your hooks, and you'll notice that you're losing fewer fish. At the very least, try it when you find you're losing a lot of fish.

Bodkins

A bodkin is a needle with a handle. It's a fly tying tool with many uses. I carry one in my vest pocket for loosening knots and tangles and clearing the eyes of fly hooks which sometimes become clogged with head cement. Its length and handle make it easier to use than the short needle which is sometimes found on a pair of nippers.

> ***Safety Tip***
>
> *Since a bodkin is sharp, it can be difficult to carry safely. I have resolved this by sheathing the needle end in a small piece of fish tank tubing which makes it safe to carry in my vest pocket.*

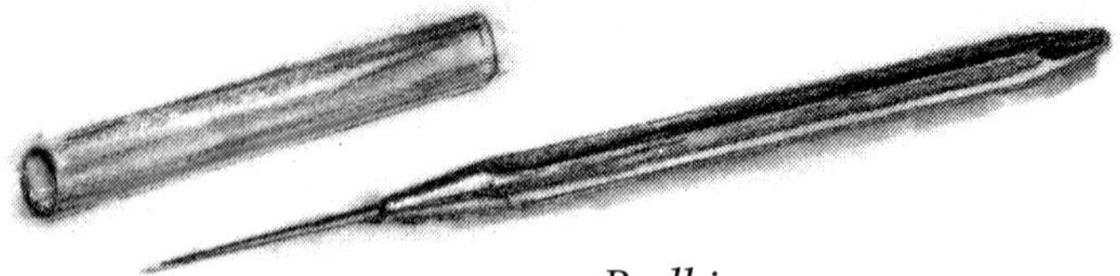

Bodkin

Creels

If you're going to keep fish you will need a creel. Traditional basket creels require keeping wet grass inside them in order to create cooling through evaporation. They work well and are romantic looking but I think the wet grass thing is a bit of a pain and I find them somewhat bulky. Modern creels are usually made from canvas. Some have waterproof liners while others are designed to be kept wet in order to maintain coolness, again through evaporation. Most of these have a waterproof flap on the side which rests against your body. If you choose one of these, make sure it does.

I use a Swiss army surplus medical bag. It's made from a waterproof rubberized canvas and is just about the right size to hold two or three decent size trout. They are very inexpensive and make a great little creel.

Polarized Sunglasses

Forming a strategy for catching fish with a fly very often involves seeing the fish and how they behave, as well as seeing how they react to the presentation of your fly. Polarized sunglasses cut the glare and enable you to see more clearly into the water.

They are an essential tool for fly fishing. Although they can be costly, the less expensive ones work just fine. If you wear prescription glasses, consider clip-ons which are quite affordable.

> *Making a decision about what equipment to buy when you first start out can be difficult. If you're on a budget, it's somewhat easier. You just buy what you can afford. If you have some means, the choice gets harder. Buying the best you can afford is not always the answer. First of all, more expensive is not necessarily better. Secondly, there's something to be said for starting out with less expensive gear, feeling it out, and then making a decision. Sometimes, you find something inexpensive that works just fine for you. If not, at least you didn't*

pay a lot for the opportunity to try it out. If you decide later to trade up you can either keep your original purchase as a back-up or pass it on to someone who's starting out.

Care And Maintenance Of Equipment

A few simple maintenance procedures will keep your equipment functioning well and will increase its lifespan.

Rods

Fly rods are delicate and can break easily. Unless there is some sort of defect in the blank, they don't usually break when fighting fish. They are more likely to be broken by a closing car trunk lid on them or by being caught in a door. Be aware of these potentially hazardous situations and take extra care when transporting a rod into the car or house. A safer bet is to break down the rod and stow it in a tube before taking it anywhere. Another dangerous and embarrassing situation is when you leave your rod on top of the car while getting ready to go somewhere and forget it was there and drive off. This is just pure stupidity. I know, because I've done it!

How to carry a rod through woods or brush is one of those great fly fishing debates. Some advocate pointing the rod behind you and others pointing it forward. They advocate each under very specific circumstances which I can't remember and most likely neither will you. You may try either method and see what's comfortable for you, but if you really don't care to take any chances with your favorite fly rod, break it down. It only takes a minute to break down a 2 or even a 4 piece rod and it's a lot more comfortable to carry it that way through heavy brush.

When stowing a rod in a compartmentalized sock, face each section so that the thinner part is facing the thicker part of its neighbor. This is a little extra precaution that will help protect the rod.

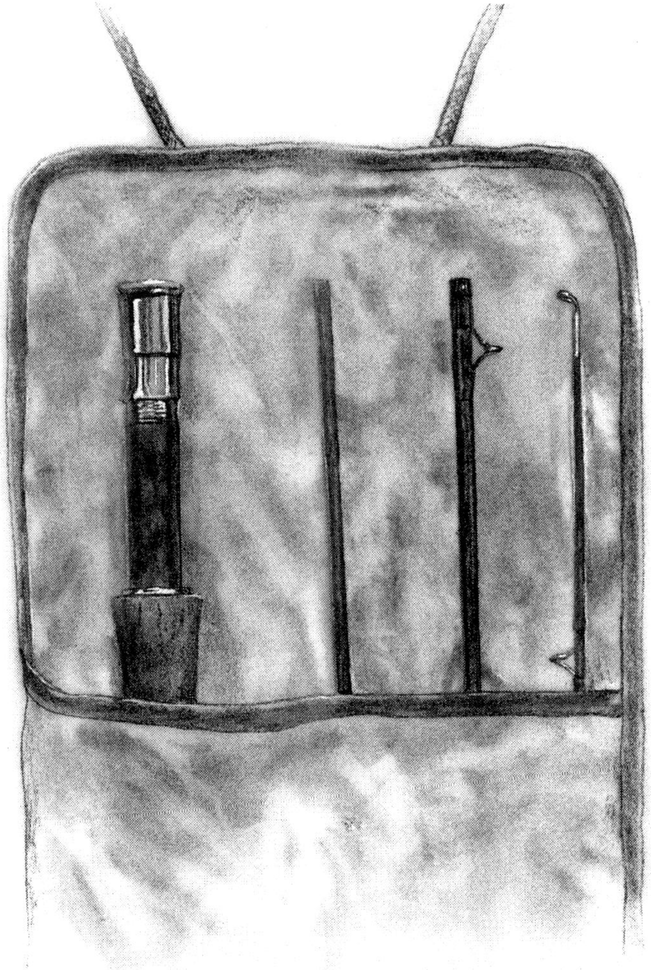

Stowing Order Of Rod Sections

Rods should be rinsed in fresh water – especially when used in saltwater – and occasionally washed with mild soap or dishwashing liquid. Make sure your rod is thoroughly dry before you put it back into its sock or case. A damp rod can develop mildew which can damage guide wrappings and generally be problematic.

Very dirty cork handles can be cleaned with rubbing alcohol. Chipped cork can be filled with a filler mixed with cork dust, allowed to dry and than sanded very lightly. Cork fillers can be purchased at tackle stores that carry rod building supplies or mail order rod building companies.

> *After washing and drying I like to use Armor All® protectant or a similar product to protect the rod. A coating of this on the guides reduces friction and helps the fly line shoot through the guides.*

Reels

Reels should always be rinsed with fresh water again, especially when used in saltwater. Remove the spool and rinse with a light flow or spray rather than high pressure. High pressure can force salt or debris deeper into the mechanism. This is really more important with spinning reels which are more complicated, but it's still a good precaution with a fly reel. Allow the reel to dry thoroughly before you assemble it.

Lubricate your reel at least once a season or whenever it feels as though it needs it. A small amount of reel lubricant on the shaft is all it takes. It's a good idea to spray a reel with a lubricant such as WD-40® before using it in saltwater, especially if it wasn't designed for saltwater use.

Line

Line should be washed often with mild soap or dishwashing detergent. Strip the line into a bucket of soapy water in carefully laid out coils, let it soak a while, then rinse it well and spool it back onto the reel. Allow the line and reel to dry well before returning it to its case. I used to coat my line with a protectant, but I find the newer lines not only don't require it but seem to do better without it.

Casting a line on the grass is not good for it! Grass creates small abrasions in your line. This is a bit of a problem because the grass is a good place to practice. Large, open fields of grass give you the advantage of having no obstacles and plenty of room for your cast. They are good places to learn and practice without becoming distracted.

Some instructors maintain that this is the only place to really learn how to cast. I believe in doing both. Some casts, like the roll cast, can only be done properly on the water. The lawn serves best as an extension of the classroom and a laboratory. It's a great place to start or to hone particular skills. Eventually you're going to have to learn to cast on the water. That's where the fish are.

One of the main premises of this book is to keep your expenses down, so I'm not going to tell you to buy two lines, but if you have an old line, you may want to set it aside for casting on the lawn.

After a few seasons of hard fishing, a line will wear. It will become abraded and rough and will no longer shoot through the guides easily. At this point, it should be replaced. A good indication of a worn line is that you begin to notice your casts decreasing in distance and generally requiring more effort for less results. At first you may suspect that you're doing something wrong. This may be the case. Sometimes we slip into bad casting habits without realizing it. It's good to be self critical, but before you start beating yourself up, check your line.

Wading Equipment

Waders, wading shoes, jackets, belts and staffs should be washed with dishwashing detergent, rinsed with fresh water and allowed to dry thoroughly before packing them. Wading shoes especially tend to pick up a lot of dirt and should be well scrubbed with a stiff brush.

> *Due to concerns about the spread of aquatic nuisance species and diseases, many now recommend sterilizing your wading equipment, especially when fishing different bodies of water.*
>
> *Recommendations for sterilizing your equipment run from soaking them in various solutions of salt, bleach, ammonia, household cleaning products, and chemicals, to freezing or heating them. Research has been complicated and results as to effectiveness and possible damage to the equipment is confusing and unclear. I would suggest contacting your local environmental agency for their opinion of how best to implement these procedures. Whether you choose to sterilize or not, thorough cleaning and drying of wading items is a good idea, both for the preservation of the resource and your equipment.*

Flies

Any flies used in saltwater should be rinsed thoroughly with fresh water. All flies should be allowed to dry thoroughly. This is often accomplished by simply leaving your fly boxes open for a while. If they look shabby after they dry, you can help restore them by holding them (with a pair hemostats, tweezers or pliers to prevent the possibility of scalding yourself) over a steaming tea kettle and preening them back into shape.

Maintenance is generally a matter of keeping things clean and dry. The best way to accomplish this is to discipline yourself to take care of your equipment immediately after you arrive home. There have been many times when after a hard day on the water, I just wanted to go to bed, but forced myself to take care of my equipment and was later glad I did. If you put it off till the next day, it just becomes harder to face the task and, if you're like me, you risk the possibility of forgetting to do it at all.

Largemouth Bass

Spooling The Reel

Before you spool up your reel you need to decide whether to set it up for right or left-handed retrieval.

This is another controversial subject. In America we generally wind the reel with the hand which is not holding the rod. This is convenient because you can just reach down to the reel handle and begin to crank. In England, they traditionally switch the rod to the other hand and reel with their strong hand. (They also drive on the left hand side of the road, call a toilet a loo and drink warm beer.)

Some experts claim that this is proper because you need the extra strength allotted to your strong hand to reel in the fish. I maintain this is only a factor when battling a very large fish.

Of more importance here is individual comfort level. Most people will be more comfortable retrieving with the hand which does not hold the rod. Others like to switch the rod to the other hand and reel with the strong hand. Neither is right or wrong. Choose whichever method feels more comfortable and natural to you. Most reels can be adjusted for either right or left-handed retrieval. Ask someone who knows to help you set up this function and teach you how to do it. Be aware that some older reels only retrieve in one direction. If you have such a reel, you'll have to adjust to it.

The average fly line is about 90 feet long. That means it won't completely fill the spool of the reel that's intended to hold it. In order to fill that spool we use backing. Fly line backing is braided Dacron® line. It usually comes in strengths of 20 to 30 pounds.

If you buy your line and reel at a store, you may ask them to spool it up for you. Since most fishing tackle stores have an automatic line winder, they usually know from experience how much backing is needed to help fill a certain reel with a particular line, so this is an easy task for them.

If you wish to do this yourself, here's my method. It's not difficult to do and keeps you from having to rely on someone else.

First, spool the fly line onto your reel front end first. Since this is just a temporary method of determining how much backing you will need, you can start it on the spool by simply winding the line over itself.

Next, attach the fly line to the backing with an Albright Knot. Although there are a couple of knots that can be used for this, I find the Albright Knot the easiest to tie and one of the most effective.

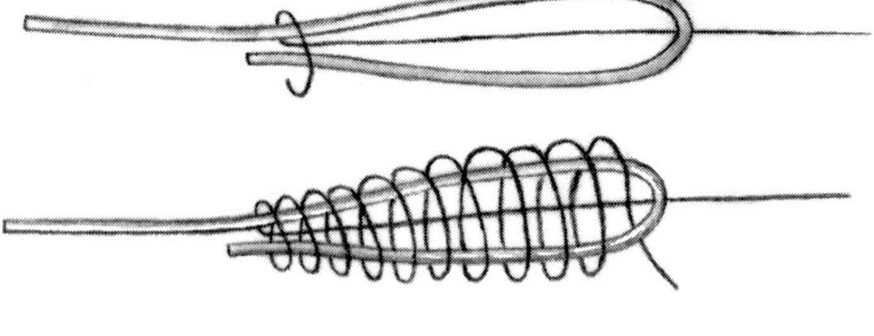

Albright Knot

Continue to wind the backing onto the spool until you fill the reel to about ¼" from the top.

You now have the proper amount of line and backing to fill the reel. The question is, how do you get it off the reel and back on in the right order? Unless you have another identical reel or extra spool, you're in trouble because if you take it off by winding it onto a different reel, when you rewind it back onto the original reel, you'll be right back where you started.

Okay, here's a method I devised for dealing with this situation. First you need a cylinder of some kind. A wide cardboard tube is ideal, but if you can't find one, a section of PVC tubing, a water or soda bottle, or even a rolled up newspaper or magazine held with tape will do.

Here's how to proceed. You've spooled the line and backing onto the reel in reverse order, filling it to about ¼" from the top. Now, take the end of the backing and adhere it to your cylinder with a piece of masking tape. Coil the backing and line onto one end of the cylinder in neat coils. Make sure you don't overlap the coils.

With your line and backing laid out in coils alongside one another on the cylinder, you are now able to access the backing from one end of the cylinder and spool it on the reel in the proper order.

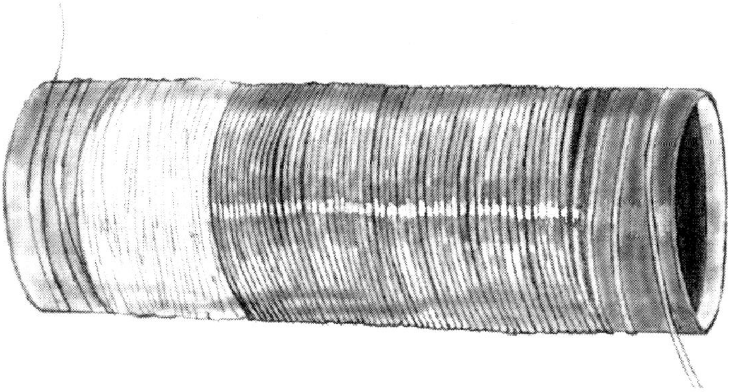

Fly Line Wrapped On Cylinder

Since you have already determined the proper amount of backing, the reel will now be filled to the right height on the spool.

This method takes a little patience, but it's effective. Others suggest just laying your line down in large loose coils in a bucket or similar container. I've tried this method and I don't like it.

As heavy and simple as fly line is, it can still tangle and bird's-nest just like monofilament. Granted, this predicament doesn't happen as often as it may with mono. The difference is that the frustration of a bird's nest of monofilament is easily resolved by taking a pair of scissors and sacrificing fifty yards or so. This is not an option with a fly line.

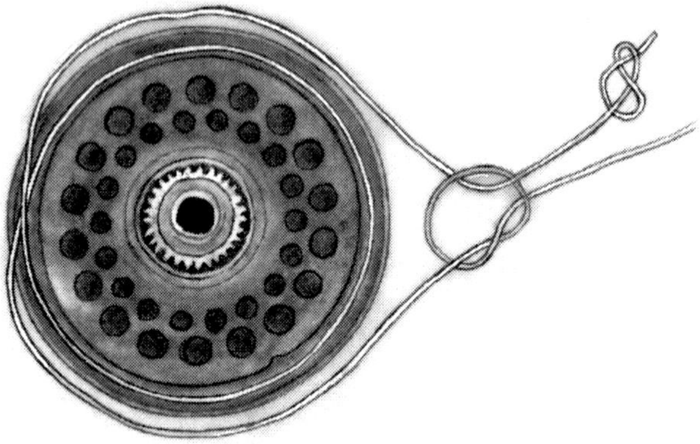

Attaching Backing To Reel

Threading The Line Through The Guides

You may thread the line through the guides with or without the leader attached. This seems like a simple procedure which doesn't require much of an explanation, but passing the thin tippet section or even the end of the fly line with the loop connection attached can be a little awkward. A fly rod has a lot of guides. If you accidently let go of the line while threading it this way it will drop back through the guides in a nanosecond, leaving you to start all over again.

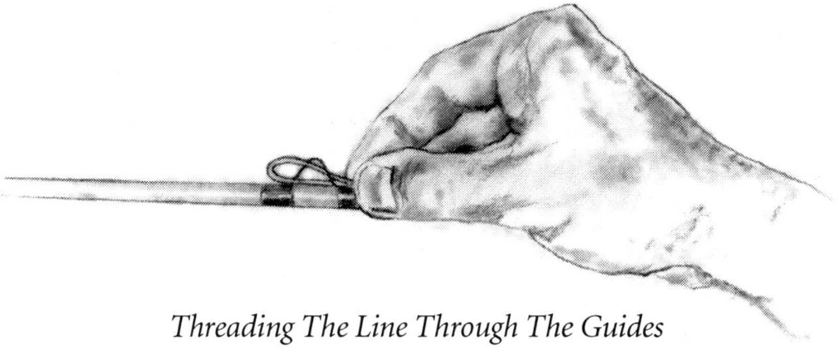

Threading The Line Through The Guides

Here's what to do. A couple of feet back from the end, fold the fly line over itself, creating a loop in the line. Thread this loop of fly line through the guides. It will be much easier to handle than the straight line or leader. More importantly, if you let go of it, the looped line will not drop through the guides. It will stop and prevent you from having to start re-threading it all the way from the first guide.

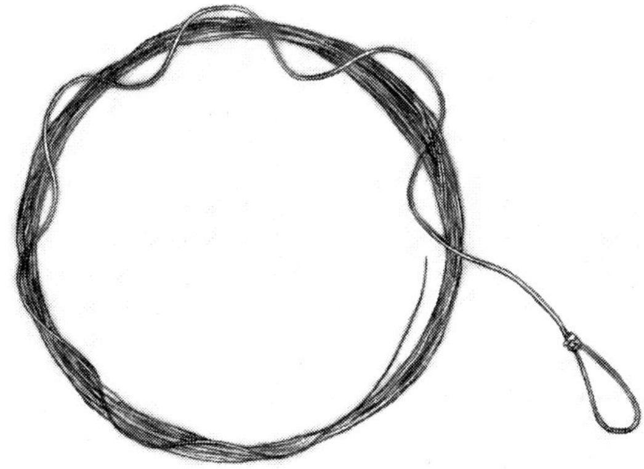

Leader As Stowed In Package

Preparing The Leader

Leaders usually come two in a package. Each is coiled in a circle about 2" in diameter. In order to keep the leader coiled, the last few inches of the butt section is snaked around the coil. Carefully unwind the butt section first, then the main coil, otherwise you'll tangle it into a bird's nest and render it useless.

Monofilament has memory, which means it maintains the form it has been shaped into. After the leader is uncoiled it will still be slightly curled. To straighten it, simply stretch a section of about a foot or so at a time. Do not pull the leader through your fingers. This causes the mono to heat up and weakens it. There are a few devices sold as leader stretchers. They are not necessary. Don't waste your money.

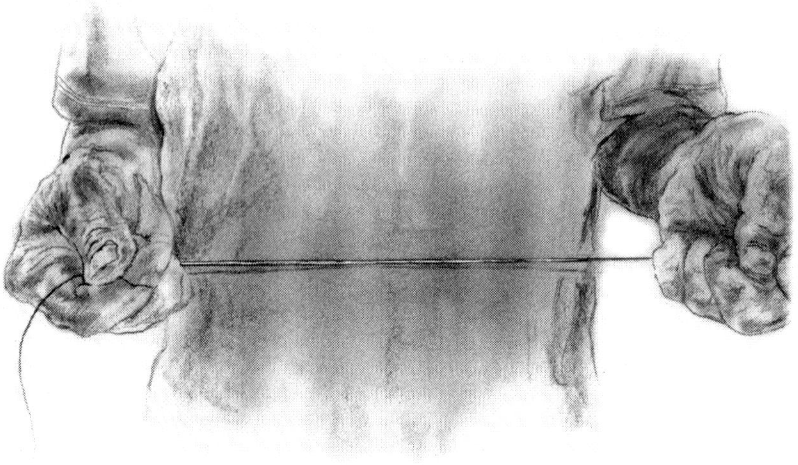

Straightening A Leader

Leader To Line

Now that your backing and line are spooled up, the next step is to attach your leader to your line. The best way to do this is by using a loop-to-loop connection.

Most fly lines now come with either a braided loop connector or a monofilament loop connector already attached to them. Most leaders also come with a loop already tied at the butt end of the leader.

If your leader does not have a loop or for some reason you need to replace it, you can tie one using either a surgeon's loop or a perfection loop.

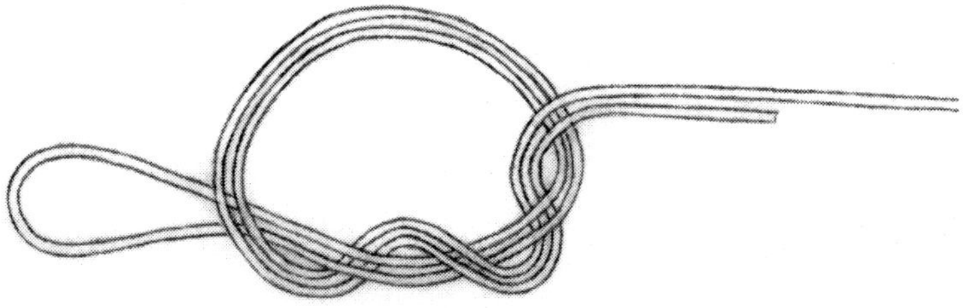

Surgeon's Loop

If your fly line and leader have these loops, simply slip the loop which is on the leader through the loop connector on the fly line. Now take the end of the tippet and pass it through the loop on the leader. Pull it though all the way and you have a loop-to-loop connection. When you're finished, it should look like a square knot. The loop-to-loop connection has the advantage of being taken apart and put back together easily and quickly.

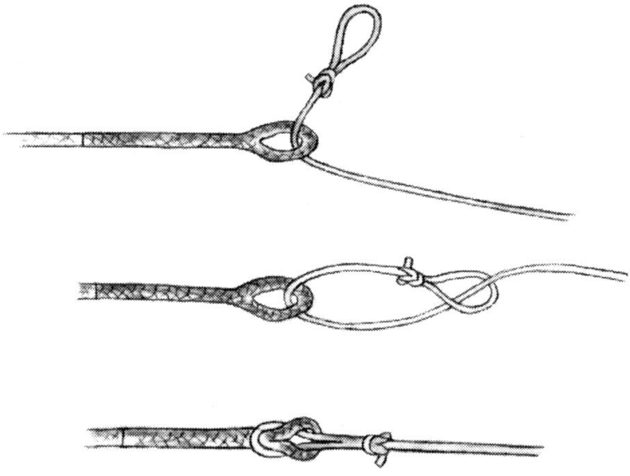

Loop-To-Loop Connection

If your fly line doesn't come with a loop attached to it you can attach one.

Braided loop connectors usually come in packs of three. It's a little tricky to attach, so you may want to have someone demonstrate the procedure to you. Your local fly shop salesperson will most likely be more than glad to show you how it's done.

A braided loop connector is made from nylon braided tubing. If you're old enough to remember, there used to be a dime store gag item known as "Chinese Handcuffs." It was basically a tube about 6" long made of woven flat basket straw. If you put a finger in each end of the tube and pulled, you discovered that you were handcuffed. The more you pulled your fingers apart, the more the tube tightened around your fingers. In order to get loose, you had to push your fingers together so that the tube expanded and you were able to free your fingers.

The braided loop connector works on the same principle. You insert the end of your fly line into the open end of the loop connector. Pushing the end of the connector toward the loop causes it to open. Once the fly line is in, you can pinch the end of the connector together with the tips of your fingers and inch-worm your way up the fly line till it's in about an inch or so. Then there's usually a piece of plastic tubing which goes on the fly line first and slips over the open end of the loop to hold it in place.

Braided Loop Connector

A monofilament loop connector is another option. This is simply a piece of monofilament of about 40 lb. test which is attached to the fly line with a Nail Knot. It runs about 4" in length and ends with a Perfection Loop.

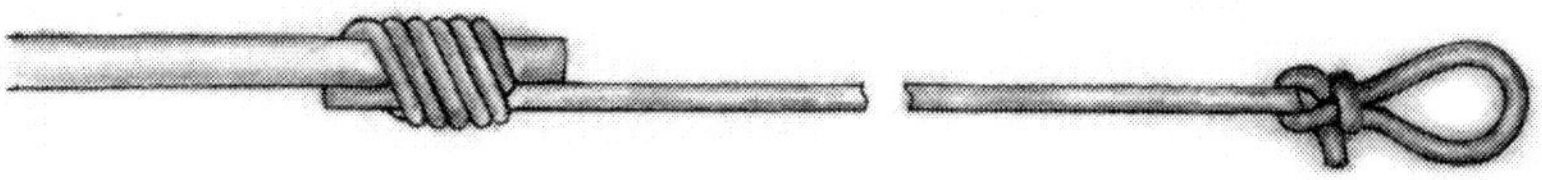

Monofilament Loop Connector

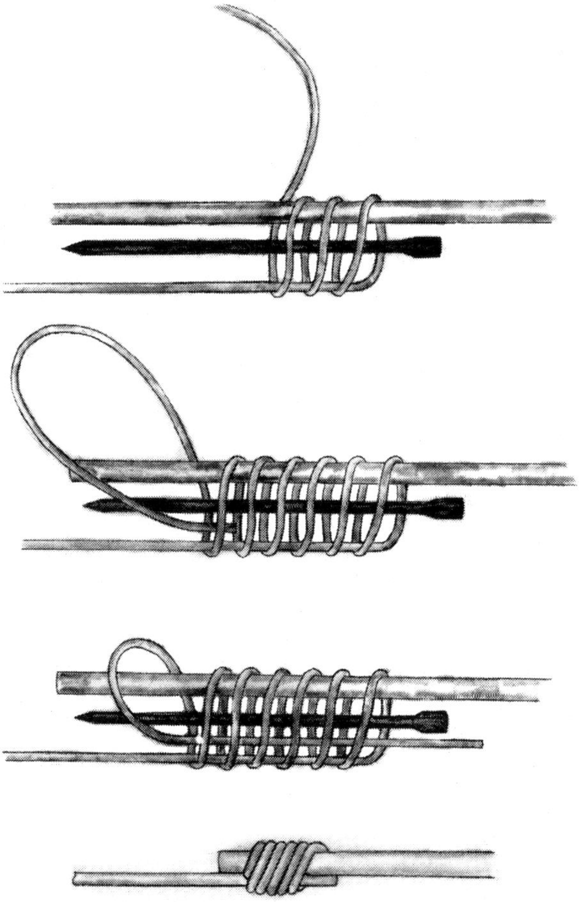

Nail Knot

This connector has one small advantage over the braided connector. The braided loop connector may fray after a while, whereas the 40 lb. monofilament is pretty tough stuff and will probably last as long or maybe longer than your fly line. On the other hand, the monofilament loop connector requires tying a Nail Knot and a Perfection Loop which are good skills for the fly fisher to have, but are a little complex and not necessary to know when you're first getting started.

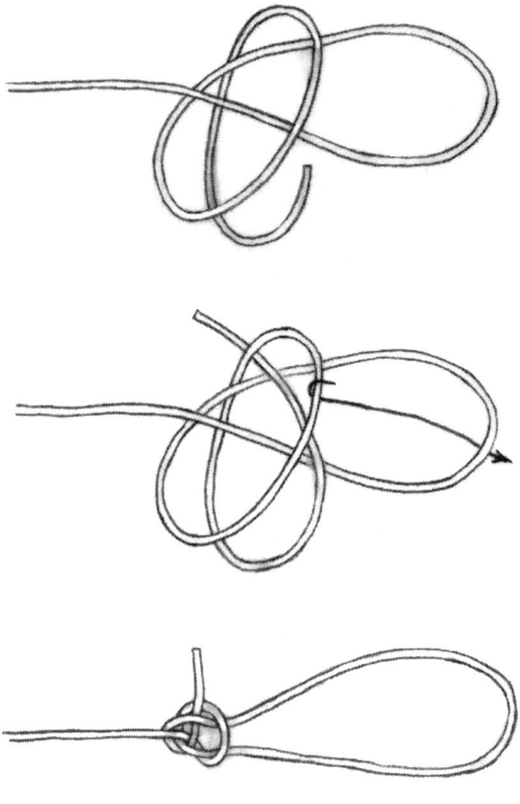

Perfection Loop

> *There is yet another option for connecting fly line to leader when the fly line does not have a loop. The fly line may be connected directly to the leader with a nail knot. This is a neat and direct connection but it requires re-tying the nail knot each time you change your leader. I would recommend that a beginner use a loop-to-loop system for the line-to-leader connection.*
>
> *Chances are the fly line you purchase or acquire will already have a loop of one kind or another at the end of the fly line. If it doesn't and you need to create one, it would be best to seek help from someone who knows the drill and can both rig it up correctly and also teach you how to do it yourself in the future.*

Replacing The Tippet Section Of The Leader

If you've changed your flies a number of times and the tippet section of your leader has become too short (less than around 16"), your presentation will become less delicate and most likely less effective. This is when you need to add a new length of tippet to your leader.

Spool off a length of tippet material longer than you need. This will leavc you some margin for error. You can shorten it later if need be. Tie it to your leader using a Surgeon's Knot.

A Blood Knot is used for making leaders by tying together pieces of mono in gradually thinner diameters. It may be used for this connection, but it's more difficult to tie, and a Surgeon's Knot will do the job just fine.

Naturally, after you replace your tippet section a couple of times you'll be into a thicker part of the leader and will eventually want to replace it entirely.

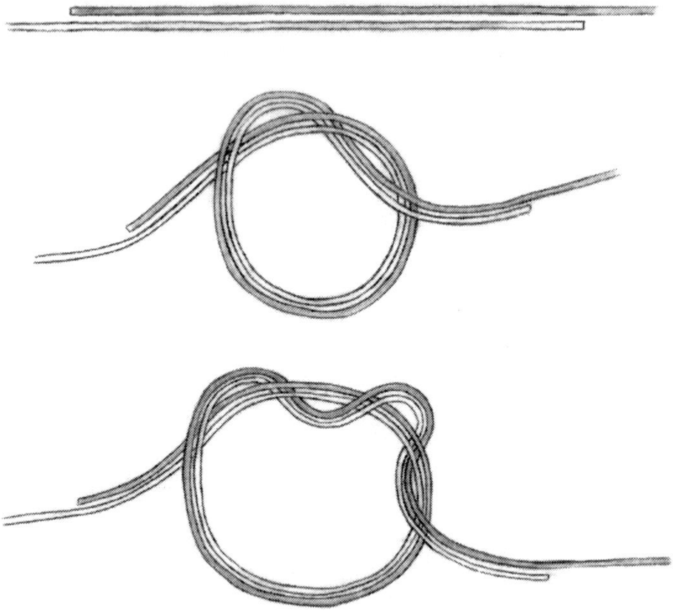

Surgeon's Knot

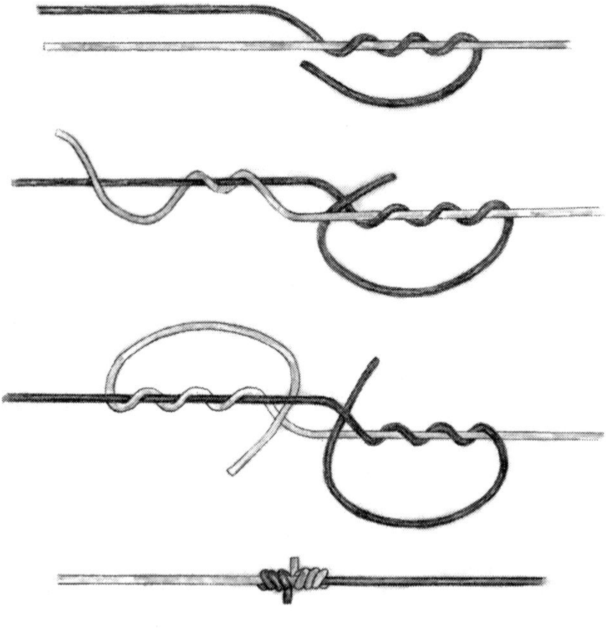

Blood Knot

Fly To Tippet

You're now ready to tie on a fly. There are at least a half a dozen or so knots that you can use for this. The Improved Clinch Knot is one of the easiest to tie and one of the most effective for this task.

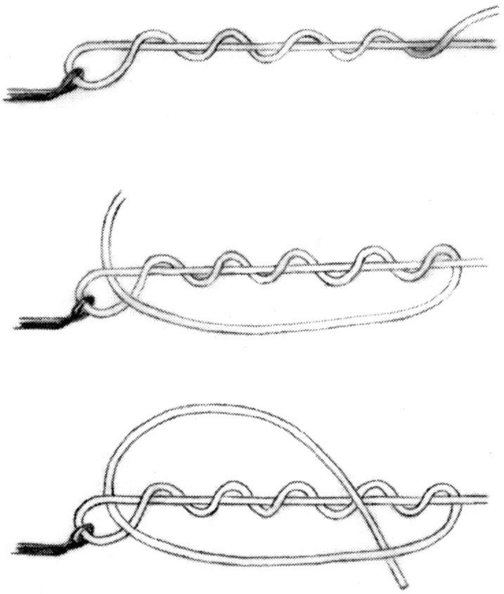

Improved Clinch Knot

There are three steps to take when tying a knot:

1. *Form the knot.*
2. *Tighten the knot.*
3. *Test the knot.*

Always wet a knot tied with monofilament before you tighten it. Monofilament heats from friction and weakens if it's tightened when dry. Your saliva is the handiest wetting agent for this job. If you're too squeamish to do this, maybe you should consider golf.

Always check all of your rigging connections and your leader to make sure they are properly tied and not worn. A frayed leader or a loose or badly tied knot can easily result in a lost fish. Odds of chance will cause you to lose enough fish, so you should stack the odds in your favor by being diligent in your rigging procedure.

In this chapter, I have shown you all the knots that are necessary for rigging up a fly line, from attaching the backing to the reel right up to tying the fly onto the tippet. In many cases some of these knots will either be pre-tied on the materials when you purchase them, or tied for you by the sellers. Eventually it would be a good thing to learn these knots, but it's not necessary when you're first starting out.

You can start fly fishing by knowing three knots: the Improved Clinch Knot, the Surgeon's Knot (and the Surgeon's Loop which is a simple variation) and the Loop-To-Loop Connection. These three are simple knots that can be learned in ten minutes. Don't let this stuff scare you!

Smallmouth Bass

In order to be able to cast a fly rod, you must understand the principle upon which fly casting is based. Casting, whether it be a with a fly rod, a spinning or a casting rod, works on the principle of stored energy. Think of a bow and arrow. You bend a bow using your bodily strength. The energy is stored until you release the string and launch the arrow. A fishing rod works the same way. It must bend (load) to store the energy and then it must unbend (unload) to deliver the cast.

In order to load, some form of weight must be applied to the line. With spinning and casting rods a sinker, lure, or even a heavy piece of bait provides the weight. In fly fishing, the fly weighs little or nothing. It is the fly line itself which provides the weight needed to cause the rod to load.

Gripping The Rod

In the basic grip, the rod is held with the thumb positioned on the top of the handle and the remaining fingers entwined around it. This is the grip you'll be using most of the time. When extreme accuracy is required, a grip placing the forefinger on top can be useful. The forefinger naturally points toward the target and helps guide the cast in that direction. There are other subtle variations which are not necessary to learn now.

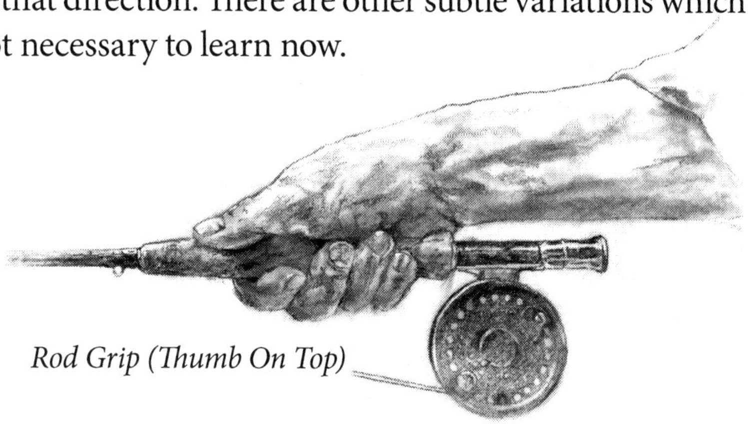

Rod Grip (Thumb On Top)

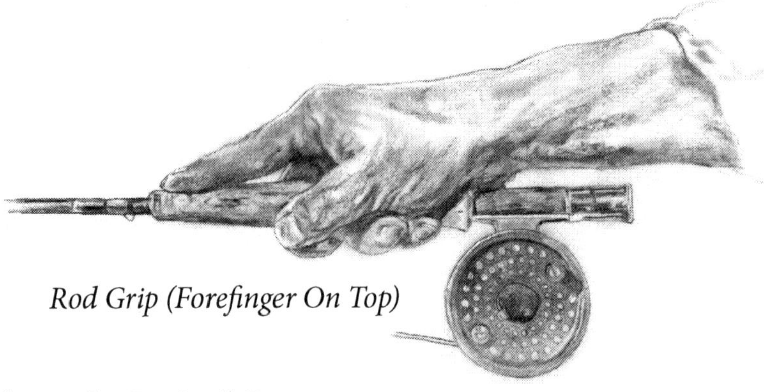

Rod Grip (Forefinger On Top)

The Pick-Up-And-Drop

There are many different casts which can be made with a fly rod. The most basic of these is the "pick-up-and-drop." In order to execute this cast properly, you must understand the principle. Since you want the rod to load, you must start with some line laid out in front of you, the tip of the rod pointed down, and **no slack line in front of you.** The resistance of the line against the water causes the rod to load. If there is slack line, there is no resistance and the rod will not load.

The first part of this cast is called the back cast. You lift the tip of the rod which begins to propel the line behind you. If you imagine the rod tip moving in the path of a clock, with 12 o'clock directly above you, you'll have a good point of reference. The rod starts to load as soon as you begin, but the maximum loading takes place approximately between the points of 11 and 1 o'clock. This is known as the power stroke area. This is where you must apply a little extra oomph. The greatest part of the loading of the rod takes place from 11 to 1 o'clock.

> *The 11 to 1 o'clock power stroke is a loose reference. There will be times when the power stroke will be wider or positioned differently, but for purposes of simplicity, 11 to 1 o'clock will serve us for now.*

At 1 o'clock, you **bring the rod to a complete stop.** The rod now unloads and propels the line in a loop in back of you until it is completely unfurled. Once the line is fully extended, you are ready to begin the forward cast.

> *Just after the stop at 1 o'clock you may follow the extended line back somewhat with the tip of your rod. This is called "drifting." The purpose of this is to create extra load on the forward cast. It's not necessary to do this now, but it's a good time to mention this technique for future reference.*

As you start the forward cast, **the rod will begin to load against the fully extended back cast.** You are now executing the power stroke for the forward cast (from 1 o'clock to 11.) At 11 o'clock you **stop the rod briefly.** The rod now unloads and delivers the line in a loop until it unfurls in front of you. After that brief stop at 11 o'clock, you immediately drop the tip of the rod back to the starting position and the line and leader falls gently on the water, delicately presenting the fly.

This is the "pick-up-and-drop." The most important things to remember are:

- Starting the cast with your rod tip pointed down and with no slack line in front of you.
- Stopping the rod at 1 o'clock and pausing long enough for your back cast to fully unfurl.
- Starting the forward cast the moment the back cast is fully extended.
- Stopping your rod again briefly at 11 o'clock.
- Immediately dropping your tip for a gentle follow-through back to your starting position.

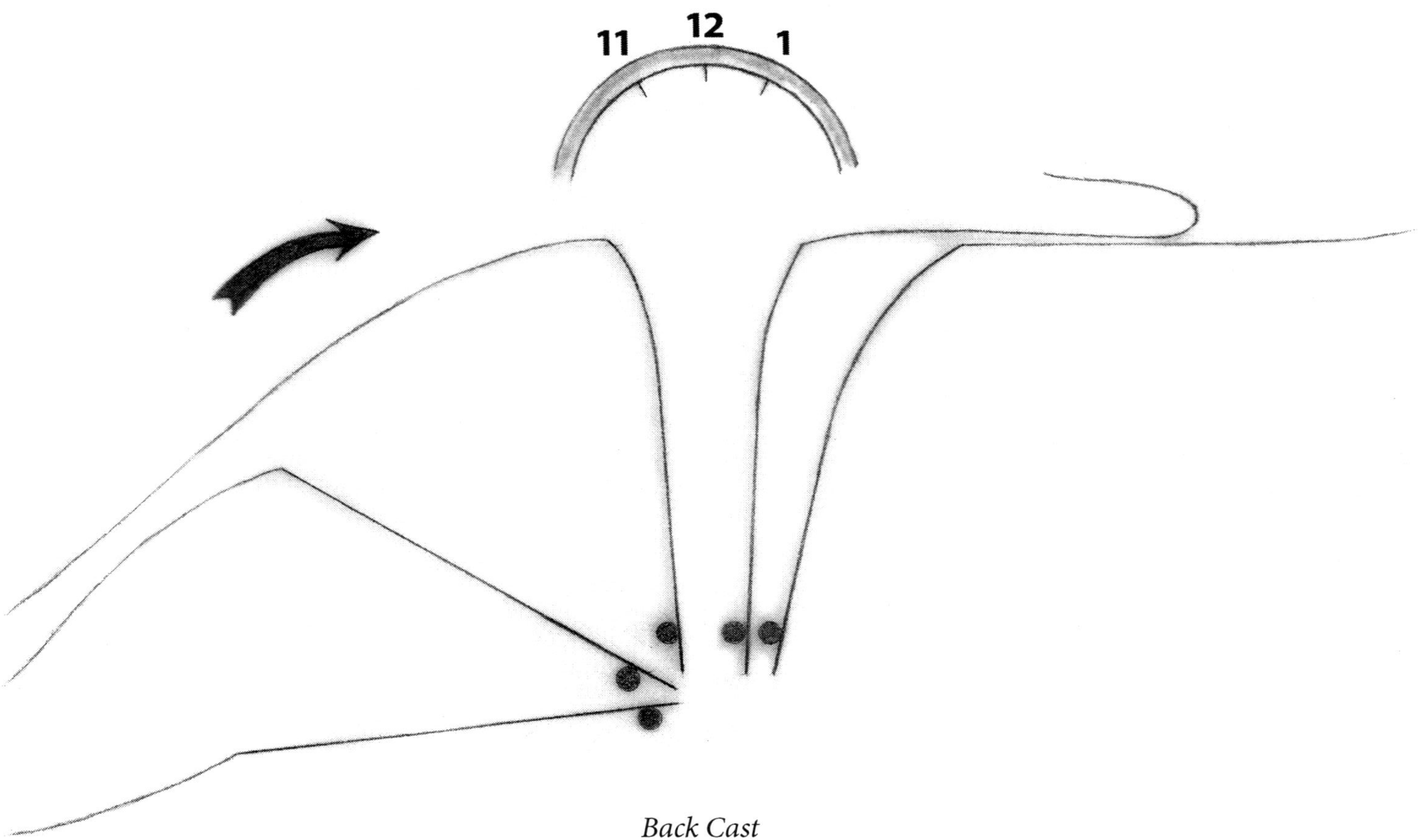

Back Cast

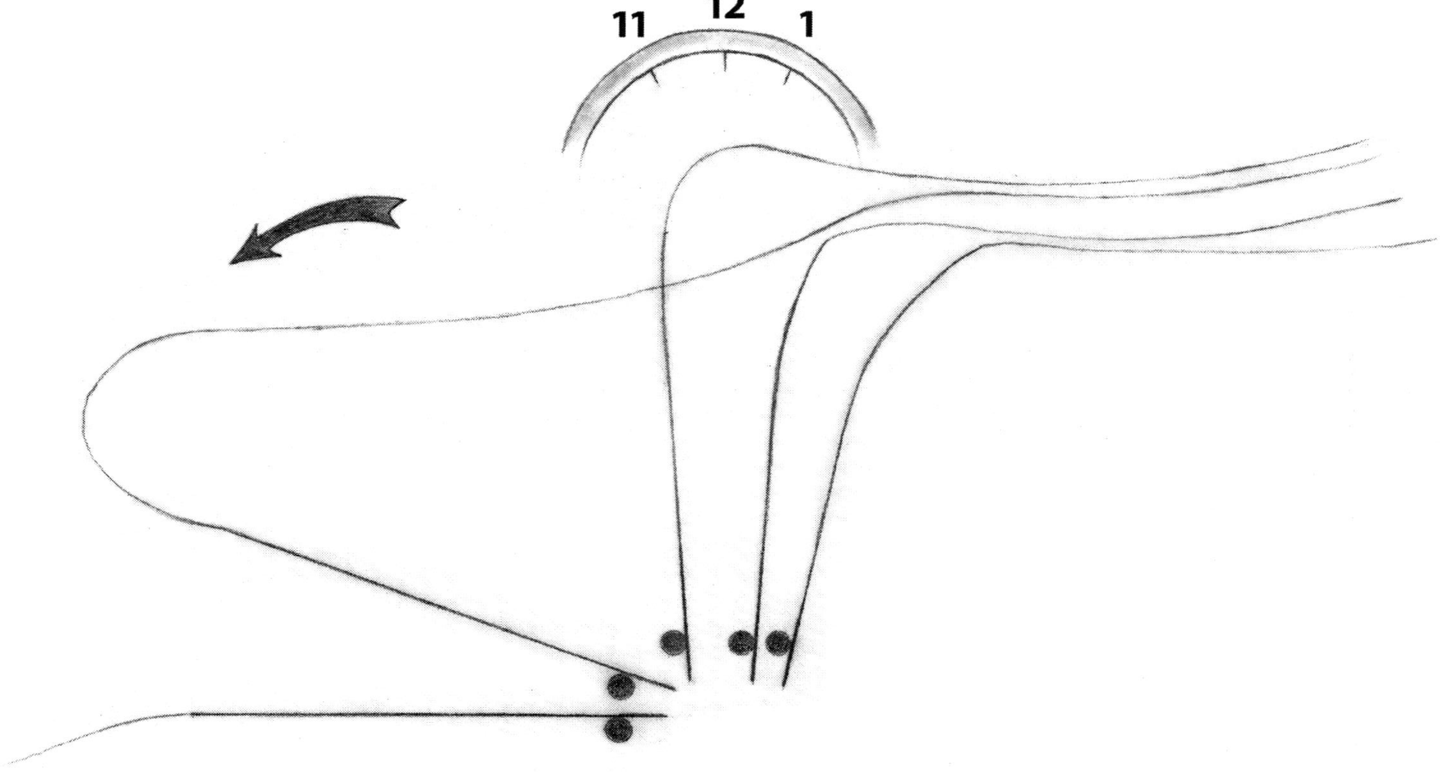

Forward Cast

False-Casting

The back-and-forth casting in the air that people generally associate with fly fishing is called false-casting or air-casting.

There are a couple of reasons to do this type of casting. One is to dry out a wet dry fly. Another is to change the direction of the cast or direct a cast to a specific target. The third is to increase line speed in order to increase the distance of your cast.

Other than these three reasons, there is no reason to false-cast, and when done unnecessarily, it is a waste of energy. However, false-casting is a great exercise for the beginner because it lets you feel the loading of the rod. The false-cast is executed within the powerstroke area from 11 to 1 o'clock and back and forth as many times as needed.

> *In order to get the rod to load to its maximum ability, the tip of the rod should move within "the casting plane." This simply means that the rod tip should move in a path which is almost parallel to the sky and the ground. This forces the rod to load.*
>
> *When we use the clock reference, we are referring to* ***the arc of the rod being created by the bending of the rod, not by swinging the rod with the wrist.*** *The wrist should be kept fairly stiff and the hand should be pushed forward slightly in order to maintain the path of the rod tip which should move almost parallel to the sky and ground.* ***Swinging the rod from the wrist is the most common cause of poor casting.***

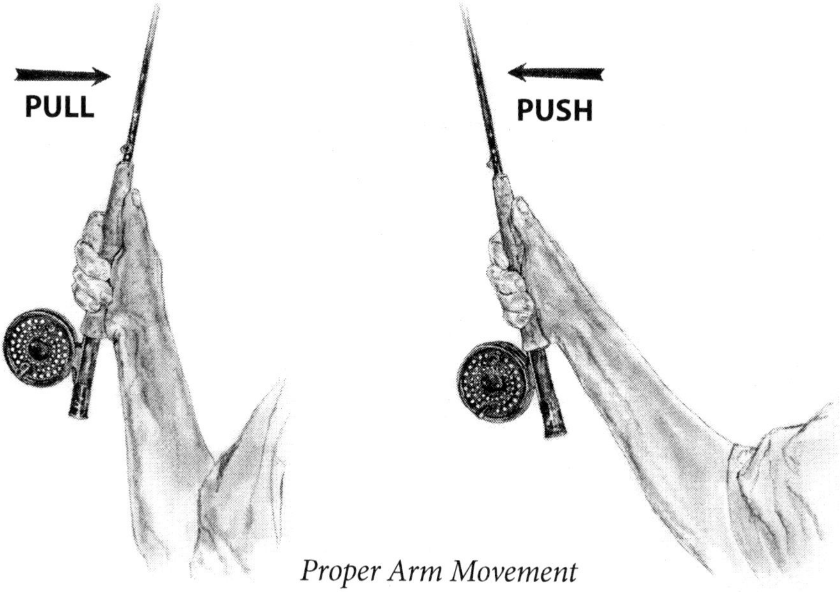

Proper Arm Movement

Strapping the butt section of the rod to the wrist will help to keep the wrist from breaking and the rod from swinging in an arc. A simple strap can be fashioned by joining 2 lengths of Velcro® tape (1 hook strip, 1 loop strip) about 1' long, back to back. If you don't have a strap, try tucking the butt of your rod into your jacket.

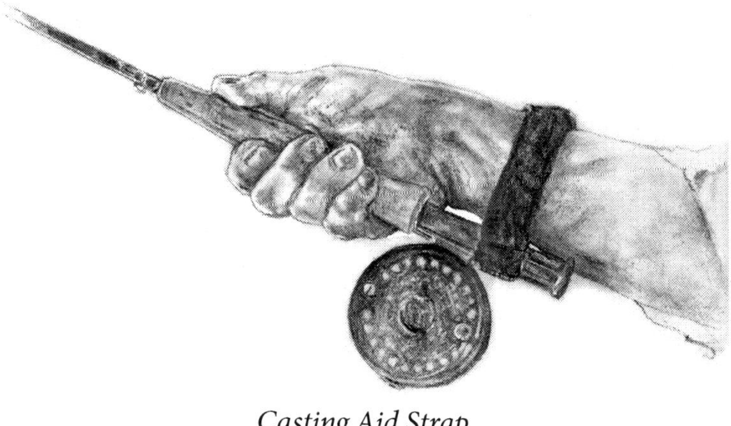

Casting Aid Strap

Roll Cast (Back Cast)

Roll Cast (Forward Cast)

The Roll Cast

This cast is an extremely important tool because the line doesn't go behind the caster and therefore enables you to cast in situations where there are obstructions behind you.

Practice the roll cast on the water. The roll cast needs to load on the water. If you try to execute it on the grass, there won't be enough resistance for the line to load the rod properly and you'll only become frustrated.

Start with some line out in front of you on the water. Always make sure your rod tip is pointed down and there is **no slack in the line in front of you.**

Slowly raise the rod tip by bending your arm at the elbow and lifting your forearm and hand. Bend your elbow and lift the rod tip until the rod is level to your ear. Make sure **the line remains on the water** during this part of the cast.

Stop the rod when it is level with your ear, then push the rod tip down toward the water, applying power as you execute this part of the cast. This is one of the few times in fly casting where a little muscle is a good thing. This movement causes the line to roll out onto the water, hence the name "roll cast."

These are the three basic casts which you need to be able to execute in order to fly fish with some degree of comfort. There are many more casts which come in handy for different situations, but you needn't concern yourself with them now. They are best learned on a need-to-know basis.

The Single Haul

In order to create more resistance and therefore load the rod more, we can use a technique called hauling. This movement is done with the hand which is not holding the rod, which is referred to as the "line hand."

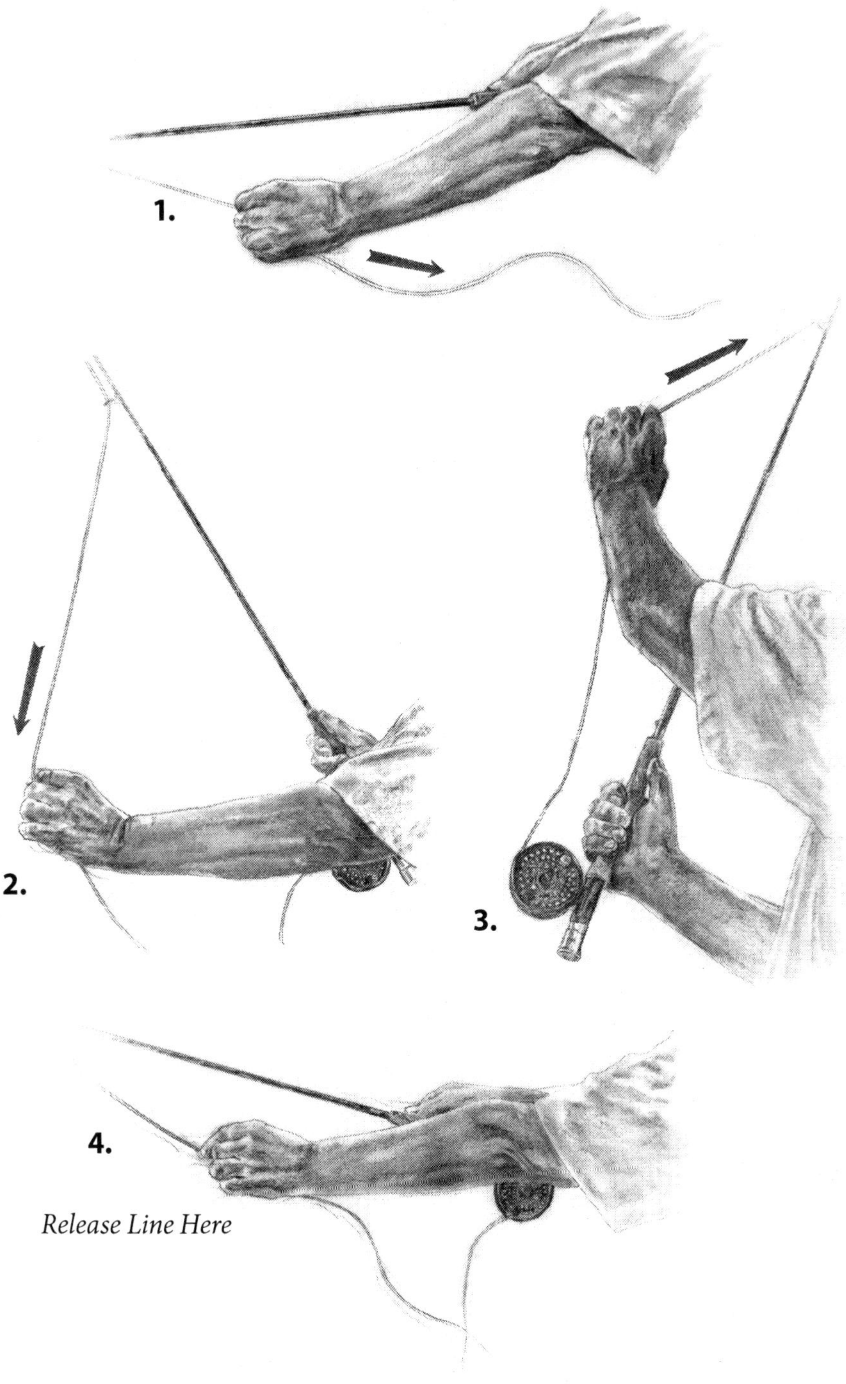

The Single Haul

First we strip some extra line from the reel, letting it drop to the ground in loose coils. This is the line we wish to shoot out as a result of the extra load we will gain by hauling.

As we begin to execute the back cast, we grip the line between our thumb and forefinger up by the stripping guide. As we raise the rod, we simultaneously haul the line toward us with our "line hand." This hauling action is creating more resistance against the line on the water. The extra tension on the line creates more load on the rod. Leaving our fingers holding the line, **we let our hand follow the line back up toward the stripping guide** as the line extends with the back cast. As we complete the forward cast, we release the line and the extra load we've created sends the line we stripped off the reel shooting through the guides and creating a longer cast.

This technique is a little more advanced and certainly not necessary to master when starting out. If you don't get it right away, don't worry, you can fish successfully without it and pick it up sometime in the future.

The Double Haul

Learning to double haul is much too advanced for the beginning fly fisher. Nevertheless, it's good to understand what it's about and to demystify it a little.

Double hauling is the big bugaboo of fly casting, thought by some to be as difficult to understand as calculus and as hard to perform as Double Dutch. It's neither.

It is simply the execution of a second haul after the first one within the same cast. The first haul is administered at the start of the back cast. The fingers continue to hold the line and follow it back up as the back cast pays out. Then the second haul is made at the start of the forward cast. It loads against the fully extended back cast.

If this confuses you, don't worry. I don't expect anyone starting out to even attempt to double haul. It falls heavily into the category of "things you don't need to be concerned with yet." For that reason I'm not even including an illustration of it. Nevertheless, some day in the future when you're ready to learn to double haul remember this: **the second haul loads against the fully extended back cast.** For now, that's all you need to know.

Stance And Body Position

Your stance should be comfortable and natural for you with your feet placed as far apart as necessary to help you feel balanced. Standing parallel to your casting direction will enable you to turn your head and observe your back cast. When first learning to cast, being able to observe and know when your back cast is fully extended may be necessary to understand when to begin your forward cast. After a while, the timing will become instinctive. This stance is generally best when making longer casts.

Facing the forward direction of your cast is generally better when making shorter casts where more accuracy is required. As you face forward, your left foot will be ahead of your right foot. (Note: if you're left-handed, your right foot will be forward.) You may rotate between these two positions in any increments you wish, depending upon the direction you wish to cast and how comfortable you feel. If extreme accuracy is your goal, place your right foot forward, pointing toward your target.

If you find yourself leaning backward to get out of the way of your cast, and losing your balance, hold your rod out at more of an angle, making your cast less directly overhead and a little more side-armed.

Above all, try to be as relaxed as possible. Take your time. Take breaks often. Shake out your arms and legs and stretch. A good caster makes casting look effortless. It looks that way because when it's done properly it *is* effortless.

Don't try to muscle a cast. Fly casting is one of those Zen-Tao-"go with the flow" type of activities. Even distance casting is all about timing, form and finesse first and not power alone, but how and where to apply it.

Wind

During extremely high wind conditions it may become impossible to fly cast. However, moderate wind can be dealt with. If the wind is blowing from the land toward the water it's less of a problem and it may even help your cast. Head winds blowing from the water will obviously be working against you. Here are some things that may help you:

- Wind usually comes in gusts. Try to time your casts so that they are delivered between the gusts.
- Instead of a gentle follow-through at the last part of your forward cast, punch down into the wind.
- Cast side-armed with the tip of your rod held a couple of feet off the ground. This will often allow you to cast under the strongest part of the wind. This cast is executed exactly the same as the overhead cast except the rod tip is held lower.
- Try developing greater line speed by hauling.

There are other, more advanced casting techniques for both headwind and winds from other directions. They're too advanced to deal with in the beginning.

Even after you master some of these, fly casting when it's windy can be frustrating to the point of taking the enjoyment out of the experience. Sometimes it's just best to wait for better conditions.

Please bear in mind that learning to cast from written instructions falls somewhere between the difficult and the impossible.

The instructions above will best serve as a reference. Fly casting is a feeling thing and is best learned hands-on from an experienced casting instructor.

I suggest that you take some lessons if you can afford them. Instruction is usually available from fly fishing shops. Clubs and conservation groups frequently offer classes for free or at very reasonable rates and mini casting lessons are sometimes given for free at sportsmen's or fishing shows.

If none of these are available, consider asking someone whose casting you admire for a couple of pointers. Most fly fishers love to introduce someone to the sport and everyone enjoys having their ego massaged by taking on the role of expert and teacher. Bear in mind that not everyone is a good teacher. If the process seems to be going nowhere, try studying with someone else. Good chemistry is important for the learning process to work.

Sunfish

FISH AND WHAT THEY EAT

A wide variety of fish can be caught on a fly. These species are referred to by the type of water they live in: saltwater, warmwater or coldwater.

Saltwater fish which readily take a fly are: striped bass, bluefish, fluke (a.k.a. summer flounder), bonita, false albacore, weakfish, sea trout, redfish, pompano, crevalle jack, tarpon and bonefish. I'm sure there must be at least a couple of fish that I've missed.

Warmwater fish live in lakes or ponds and can survive in temperatures up to the 80s F. Those which will take a fly are: largemouth bass, smallmouth bass, crappie, sunfish, muskie, pike, pickerel, perch, carp, bowfin and again, probably a few more.

Coldwater fish are found in rivers and streams with a coldwater source and they cannot tolerate temperatures much higher than the mid-70s F. The ones which you can catch with a fly include salmon, trout, char, chub, whitefish, and grayling.

Saltwater fish feed mostly on smaller fish. They also eat worms, crustaceans and mollusks.

Freshwater species – both warmwater and coldwater – eat smaller fish. They also eat worms, crustaceans and terrestrial and aquatic insects. The more predatory of these species such as muskie, pike, pickerel, bass and large trout will eat almost anything smaller than them that happens to fall in the water. This includes mice, bats and birds. Carp are omnivorous and eat vegetation as well as insects and worms.

A major part of the diet of coldwater fish consists of aquatic insects. Aquatic insects are metamorphic. Like butterflies, they change their physical form as they grow.

There are four main categories of aquatic insects: mayflies, caddisflies, stoneflies and midges. There are numerous species of these and they all go through several stages as they mature.

Mayflies

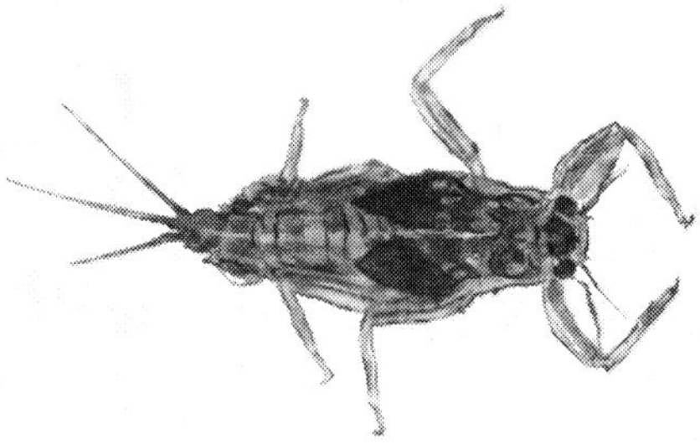

Mayfly Nymph

Mayfly Dun

Mayfly Spinner

Caddisflies

Case Caddis Larva

Caddis Pupa

Caddis Fly Adult

Stoneflies

Stonefly Nymph

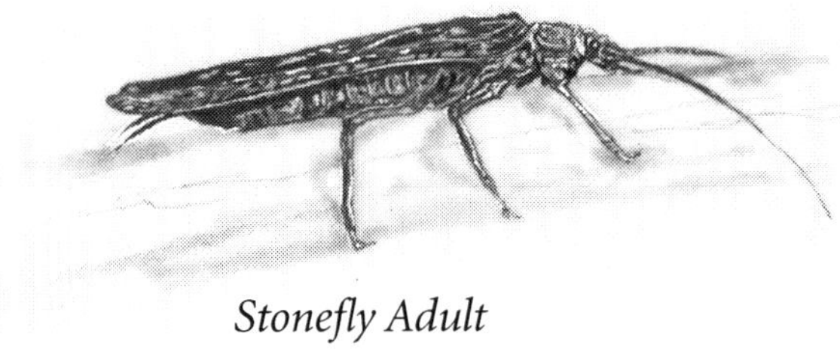

Stonefly Adult

Midges

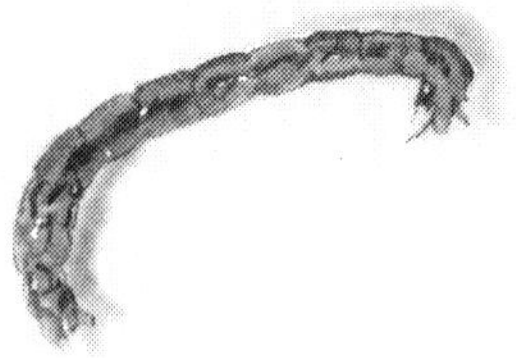

Midge Larva

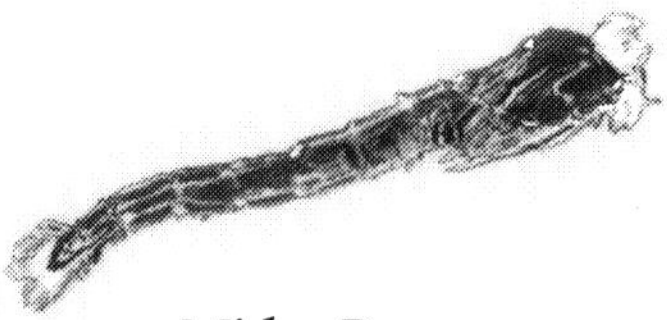

Midge Pupa

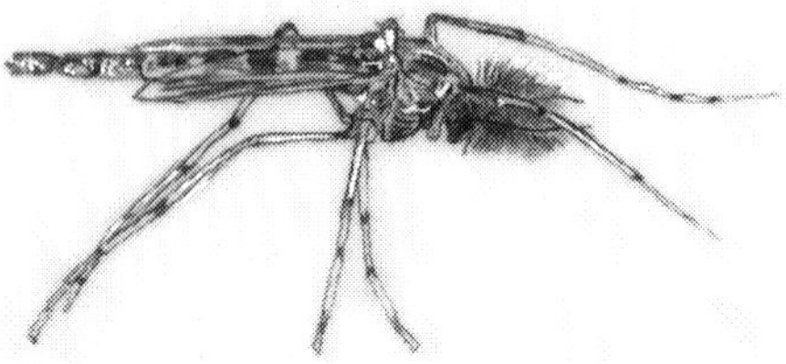

Midge Adult

Aquatic insects spend almost 90 percent of their lives in the nymphal stage. As a result of this, trout feed on the nymphal or larval stages of aquatic insects more than any of the other stages. Since nymphs dwell on the bottom, trout feed more off the bottom than at other depths of the water.

The trout's preference for aquatic insects and its tendency to sometimes zero in on one stage of a specific insect is what makes fly fishing for trout so interesting and challenging as well as sometimes frustrating or downright maddening.

Our understanding of what fish eat is a good foundation for creating the artificials we use to catch them, but it's only part of the picture.

Crappies

FLIES

Flies are categorized in several different ways. The first categorization deals with whether flies imitate something.

Those that imitate a specific food form are referred to as "imitators." Flies which make no attempt to imitate any known life form are called "attractors." Somewhere in between are a group of flies which imitate or may imitate several different food forms. These are called "broad-spectrum imitators."

A classic example of an imitator is the "Quill Gordon," which is tied to represent the living insect of that same name. A classic attractor is the "Royal Coachman," which doesn't represent anything found in nature, but seems to appeal to fish. A "Soft-Hackled Flymph," which could possibly imitate a couple of different insects, is a good example of a broad-spectrum imitator.

Quill Gordon

Royal Coachman

Soft-Hackled Flymph

Of course, this is all conjecture on our part. Until we can converse with the fish, we won't know the specific reasons why they take one fly and not another. We can only try to make an intelligent guess – which is exactly what fly fishing is all about.

Flies are also referred to by their physical characteristics. Dry flies, for instance, are flies that float on the surface, while wet flies are designed to be fished beneath the surface.

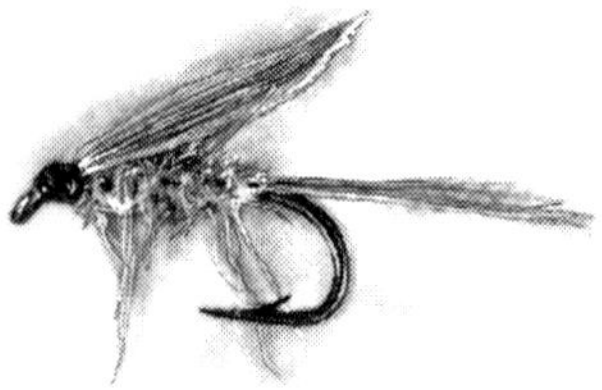

Hare's Ear Wet Fly

This categorization is mixed in with references to certain stages of an aquatic insect's metamorphosis and based on the physical habits of the insects during that stage. For instance, "nymphs" are flies that are tied to represent that early stage of an insect's development. They are usually fished on the bottom.

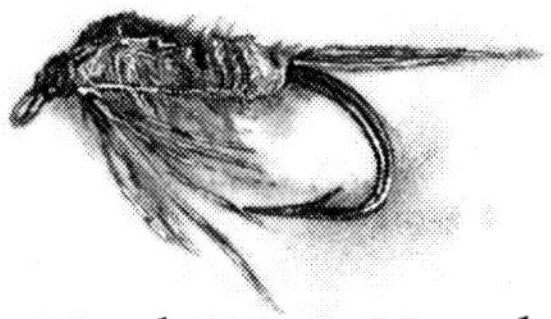

March Brown Nymph

"Emergers" are fished just beneath the surface. They represent the stage of an aquatic insect as it sheds its nymphal shuck, just before it rises to the surface to float on the water and dry its wings.

CDC Emerger

At this stage it is called a "dun." The fly tied to represent this stage is also referred to as a "dun."

Blue Winged Olive

After its wings are dry, a mayfly takes to the air, mates, lays its eggs, and falls into the water. At this stage it is called a "spinner" and so is the fly that represents it.

Rusty Spinner

Terrestrials are imitations of land-dwelling insects which fall into the water. This group of flies includes imitations of grasshoppers, leafhoppers, crickets, beetles and ants.

Ant

Streamers are fairly large flies which are tied to imitate baitfish.

Grey Ghost

Bass bugs are large, floating flies made from spun deer hair, cork, balsa wood or foam. They imitate frogs or injured fish.

Bass Bug

Saltwater flies are mostly baitfish imitations, but some are created to represent crabs or shrimp.

Lefty's Deceiver

Salmon flies are mostly fanciful attractor patterns designed to trigger a reaction (perhaps caused by anger), which creates a strike.

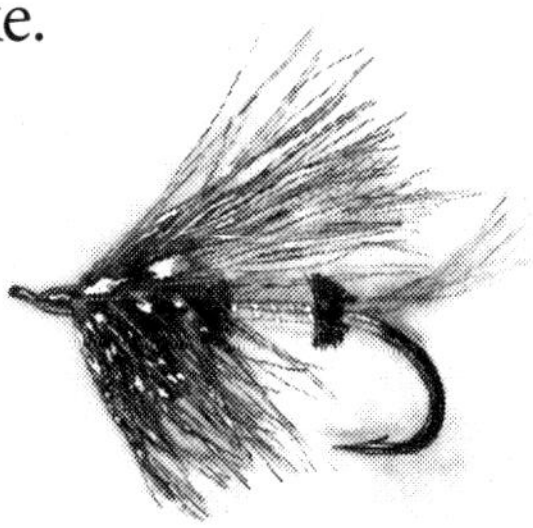

Jock Scott

Steelhead flies are either brightly-colored attractor patterns similar to salmon flies, or egg patterns that imitate fish eggs or just act as shockingly bright attractors.

Winter's Hope

Some patterns such as the extremely popular and effective wooly bugger seem to defy classification. This pattern is not really a streamer in the classical sense. It may imitate something (some claim a crayfish and others a caterpillar or hellgrammite), but is more likely just a highly effective attractor.

Wooly Bugger

These overlapping and erratic categories may seem confusing at first. Hang in there! All this will begin to make more sense once you've got some experience under your belt. Remember, there are thousands of existing patterns and countless new ones created every day. This fact itself may seem somewhat daunting, but don't let it scare you off. You can fish successfully with just a few patterns. There's more to this game than just selecting the right fly.

Fly Selection

Naturally, your selection of flies will depend on where you're fishing and which fish you're targeting. Nevertheless, here are some suggestions for a basic fly selection.

Streamers:

Wooly Bugger

Although it is not a classical streamer, the wooly bugger is presented and fished as one. It is a highly effective fly which can be used to catch trout, bass, pickerel, sunfish and occasionally even carp.

The color I prefer is yellow, but it doesn't seem very available commercially so I tie my own. Olive would be my next choice. Black is also very good. I like them tied with a cone-headed weight so they can be jigged off the bottom.

Size #6 is my first choice. One size up or down is fine.

Dry Flies:

Adams

The classical all-around dry fly, it can imitate a broad spectrum of mayflies and just may be the most effective dry fly ever fished.

Sizes #18 and #20

Elk Hair Caddis

This pattern imitates a number of different caddis hatches, is highly visible and does not require floatant.

Size #16

Griffith Gnat

This fly is my choice when fish are feeding on midges (which is most of the time.) It imitates a cluster of these tiny insects.

Sizes #20 and under

Nymphs:

Gold-Ribbed Hare's Ear

A classic all-around nymph pattern.

Sizes #16 and #18

Scud

This pattern imitates a tiny shrimp-like crustacean that is a favorite trout food. They are tied many different ways. My favorite is made with small glass beads.

Size #16

Terrestrials:

Ant

Trout love them; panfish too. An easy pattern to tie.

Size #16

So here are seven patterns that have a time-tested reputation for success. Of course, you'll want to increase your collection according to what you're fishing for and where. Notwithstanding these factors, these patterns should always be present in your fly box.

Saltwater

Since saltwater fish feed mostly on baitfish, fly selection is easier. For most northern species that take a fly (striped bass, bluefish, weakfish, shad and fluke), a Deceiver is my fly of choice. It is unweighted, but most saltwater fly fishing is done with an intermediate sink line that will present the fly sub-surface anyway.

My color preferences are chartreuse and blue.

Sizes #2 to #4

My second choice is a Clouser that is weighted for a jigging effect.

My color preference is chartreuse.

Sizes #2 to #4

You can do pretty well using these two patterns and could even get away with just one or the other.

There are of course specific patterns for the more southern species such as bonefish, pompano, tarpon, redfish, sea trout and others.

If you have a chance to fish for any of these it should be an easy matter to select flies by inquiring about them at their place of purchase.

Fly Hook Size

As numbers increase, hook size decreases until they reach #1. After #1, the larger hook sizes are indicated as #1/0, #2/0, #3/0, etc.

← smaller	larger →
etc. 8 7 6 5 4 3 2 1	1/0 2/0 3/0 4/0 etc.

Striped Bass

FISHING

Successful fishing is usually the result of understanding where the fish are and what they're eating. These two things often work in conjunction with one another.

Locating the fish depends on your knowledge of their habits and environment. This knowledge is acquired by studying the observations and conclusions of others, and by reaching your own conclusions through observation and just some plain old-fashioned trial and error.

Reading The Water

Locating fish by observing their habitat is called "reading the water." In most books on fly fishing, the chapter on "reading the water" has diagrams with little silhouettes of fish behind and in front of rocks, and here and there throughout the stream. I've always found these diagrams incredibly confusing. It reminds me of trying to learn to dance by following those diagrams of footprints with the numbers in them. Impossible!

If you understand the fishes' requirements, you'll know where to look for them in the water.

Fish seek structure. Having an object to hide behind or just relate to seems to give all living creatures a sense of security. Even we people prefer the corner table in a restaurant to the one out there in the middle.

Fish seek cover. Birds and some other predators are very real threats from above. Positioning itself under a branch or undercut bank or alongside a rock helps a fish to keep from becoming bird food.

Fish seek shelter from strong currents. Fish are programmed to expend as little energy as possible. Therefore they need their caloric intake to be greater than its expenditure. At the same time, fish seek oxygen so they may seek fast water but a sheltered spot within it. Look for them behind, in front of and alongside rocks where the current is slow.

Fish seek food of course, so look for feeding lanes where debris and insects collect and run through the stream. Also check under overhanging branches where they get both the advantage of cover and the food supply from terrestrial insects that fall into the water.

Lastly, look for fish where they're not supposed to be, because they didn't read this book and certainly not the ones with the little diagrams.

Reading The Fish

Fly fishing, especially for trout, can be quite a visual experience. You will often see the fish you're after. Although this can be rewarding because you know that the fish are there, it can be equally as frustrating when they don't respond to anything you do.

The behavior of the fish will indicate how they're feeding and often what they're feeding on. This information is the foundation of your strategy for catching them.

If you see trout on the bottom, they're most likely feeding on nymphs. If you see the fish turning on their sides, then they are definitely feeding on nymphs.

Fish rise to the surface to feed on insects. How they rise indicates what they're feeding on. Fish making leaping rises are often feeding on caddisflies. Caddis emerge rapidly and the fish chase them accordingly. Small, quiet, gently formed rises are often caused by fish sipping insects from the surface. This type of rise may indicate that the fish are taking mayflies. Rolling, lazy rises usually mean the fish are after emerging insects. Remember that even when fish are rising, they're still usually taking nymphs beneath the surface.

Although I've been referring mostly to trout and insects they dine on, the same principles apply to other varieties of fish in both stillwater and saltwater. It all comes down to observing the behavior of the fish and trying to determine how and what they're eating.

Reading The Bugs

Even if your strategy isn't totally geared to matching the current hatch of insects, you still need to be aware of what's going on with them.

Try catching whatever is flying around, turn over a couple of rocks and check underneath or hold a small fish net in the current and see what you come up with. If you can't identify it, see what you have in your box that looks something like it. Aim for size first, then color and then general likeness.

Presentation

Presentation is the art of making an artificial lure behave in such a way that fish mistake it for real food. Most of the time, this means presenting the artificial so it behaves like the food the fish feeds on. Occasionally a fly is presented to annoy or threaten a fish in order to induce a strike. Presentation includes what type of fly is used, how it is rigged, how it is cast and how it is manipulated in the water.

Leaders And Presentation

As a general rule, leaders should be longer and tippets lighter when the water becomes clearer and the fish spookier. Of course, tippet size is relegated by the size of the fly which in turn is determined by the size of the creature the fish may feed upon.

Delicate dry fly and emerger presentations require long leaders with light tippets, sometimes as long as 12' with tippets as light as 7x or even 8x. This enables you to place a dry fly on the water gently, the way a real insect would land.

Nymphs and wet flies are usually fished with a short leader (as short as 6' depending on the conditions) in order to keep in close touch with the fly and set the hook quickly and easily.

Streamers can be fished with medium length (about 9') leaders and fairly heavy tippets (3x to 5x) in order to hold these flies, which are usually tied on larger hooks.

Always try to fish with the lightest tippet you can. If the fish start breaking off, go to a heavier size.

Presentations are sometimes referred to in terms of the type of fly being presented, such as a dry fly presentation, wet fly, nymph, emerger, streamer, etc. The following are the classical presentations associated with these types of flies.

Dry Fly

The fly is cast one-quarter upstream and is allowed to drift downstream until the fly has drifted the full length of the amount line that's been cast.

Wet Fly

The fly is cast one-quarter downstream and then it is lifted at the end of the drift to trigger a strike, perhaps because the lift imitates the action of an emerging insect.

Nymph

A small weight is tied above the fly about 12" to 18" up on the leader to help the fly stay on the bottom and straight beneath the line. Most often a strike indicator (which is really just a tiny bobber of some kind) is attached to the leader at a height which enables the fly to tumble across the bottom simulating the motion of a real nymph.

The fly is cast one-quarter upstream. As it drifts, it's followed with the tip of the rod in order to stay in close contact with the fly. When the strike indicator either stops or is pulled under, the hook is quickly set.

Emerger

Emerger imitations are constructed in such a way that they hover just beneath the surface. They may be cast and drifted in a number of different fashions. In some instances, they are left to drag for a couple of seconds at the end of the drift.

Streamer

The fly is cast down and across the stream and then stripped back upstream against the current to simulate a small fish.

These presentations are categorized by the fly which is used. Others are referred to by the waters they are used in or simply how they're done.

Stillwater and saltwater presentations deal mostly with the depth at which the fly is fished and the speed of its retrieval. There are subtle currents in stillwater and strong currents in saltwater, but neither have to be dealt with as extensively as those in a river or stream.

There are dozens of variations on these presentations: straight up and downstream dry fly, dry flies skittered upstream, nymphs fished dry, streamers presented directly cross stream, and whatever else works. This may seem incredibly complex at first. It isn't.

The best approach to learning presentation is to familiarize yourself with the basics and then get out there and toss the fly out in a couple of different ways and see what works. Every body of water has its own peculiarities and rules and these change from day to day. This is another reason why fly fishing is fun.

Presentation is the most important aspect of fly fishing. Good casting is really just a means to this end, known as presentation. Fly selection is not nearly as important. To illustrate this point, some experts fish only one fly in various sizes and concentrate solely on presentation. Needless to say, they are extremely successful.

Remember, a fish decides whether or not to take a fly in a split second. Observation and experimentation have proven that they are responding to the manner in which that fly is presented to them.

Mending

As a fly drifts down the current, the line is pulled more quickly than the leader. This causes the fly to be pulled by the line and move in an unnatural way. This phenomenon is called "drag." Although there are a couple of exceptions, for the most part, drag is bad! Nine times out of ten, fish will ignore a dragging fly because it is moving in an unnatural way.

There are a couple of casts which create slack in the line and prevent drag, but they're a little advanced to deal with in a beginner's book. Instead we'll talk about "mending" our line in order to prevent drag.

When the current starts to push the line downstream, you lift your rod in a half-circle motion upstream, like a jump-rope. This causes the line to lie in a curve upstream of the leader where it will no longer drag the fly.

The mend is a correctional procedure and may have to be repeated a couple of times during the drift as the line again begins to belly out downstream and drag the fly. This is a basic upstream mend.

Mending

Setting The Hook

Sometimes you get lucky and a fish hooks itself while taking the fly. But in most cases you need to set the hook. A fish will usually reject a fly the instant it realizes it's artificial. The time between the fish's taking the fly and rejecting it is a split second. This gives you a very small window of opportunity for setting the hook.

Try it too soon when the fly isn't quite far enough into the fish's mouth, and you'll miss. If you wait too long, the fish will spit it out. It's a timing game. Whether you see the fish taking the fly or see the strike indicator stop or go under or just feel a strike, this is the moment when your adrenaline kicks in, your heart starts to pound and your brain goes on vacation.

The only way to get good at hook setting is practice. Fishing for panfish is the ideal way to do this. Sunfish and other panfish tend to reject an artificial even more quickly than other fish, so here's an opportunity to have fun and improve your skills at the same time without worrying about losing "the fish of your lifetime."

Retrieving The Fish

After you've set the hook you obviously need to retrieve the fish. Fly fishing gives you a couple of options for doing this. As I mentioned before, the usual method for retrieving small to medium size fish is to strip them in. This is done by threading the line over the middle finger of the hand which is holding the rod, gripping the line between the thumb and forefinger of your "line hand," and pulling the line back toward you. You strip a few feet, let go of the line, move your hand back up and keep repeating the process until it is completed. If at any time during the stripping the fish starts taking line or just feels big and feisty you may opt to play the fish directly from the reel.

The advantage of doing this is that reeling the fish in is smoother than stripping and the drag feature of the reel will allow the fish to take some line, thereby relieving the extra tension which can cause the tippet to break. If you decide to put the fish on the reel after stripping, you will have to deal with the line you have stripped in. To do this, you take the line which is looped over the middle finger of your rod hand and loop it again under your pinkie. Now you are able to reel in the slack stripped line while still securing the fish. Once the slack is reeled up, you may control the fish directly from the reel.

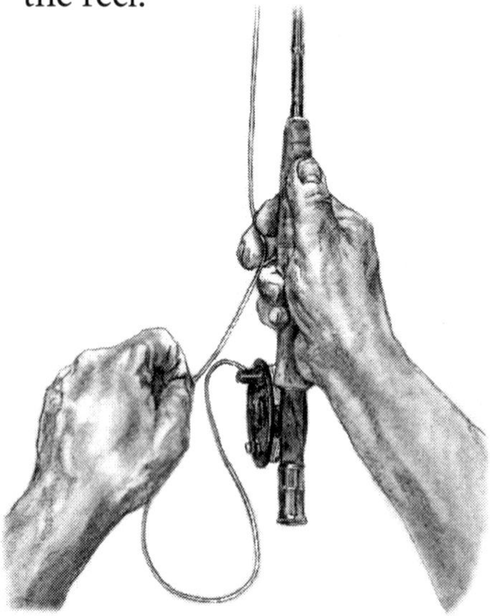

Stripping Line

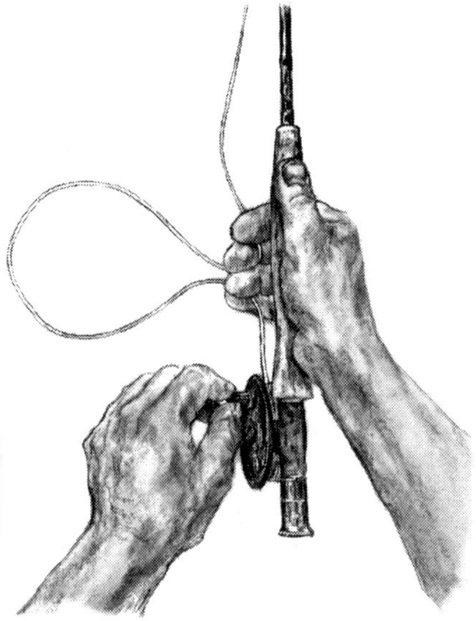

Reeling In Stripped Line

You may ask: why not just reel the fish in to begin with? Yes, this is certainly an option and seems to be more sensible, but in my opinion, stripping the fish in is more fun and the method I've described for switching from stripping to the reel gives you a choice of tactics.

As well as a method of retrieving a fish, stripping line is often used as a presentation. For this presentation a streamer fly is used to imitate a bait fish and the stripping simulates its movement. The speed of the stripping can be varied until it is effective and attracts fish.

Stripping line is also used simply as a method for getting the line back in.

Playing The Fish

When you play a fish, the idea is to apply the proper amount of tension on the line so the fish becomes tired and can be pulled in. At the same time, you don't want to apply too much tension and cause the fish to break off. It's a matter of feel, but there are a few tricks you can use to help with the task.

Pulling your rod to the side is a technique called "side pressure." It causes the fish to go on its side. This is an unnatural position that tires the fish out more quickly. Use it whenever you can when you have room enough to pull your rod to the side.

If you have the fish on the reel, don't just crank it in. Use the rod. Lift the rod tip up (or to the side) and then reel the line till the tip is down again. Keep repeating this until you are "pumping the fish in." This is a technique used by big game fishers. It works on sailfish, marlin and the like and is equally effective on smaller fish.

Fight the fish from the butt section of your rod. It's the strongest part of the rod. With this understanding in mind, never choke up on your rod. This seems to be an instinctive thing to do, but in this case, instinct stinks. Gripping your rod high up above the handle weakens it. Think about it. By doing this, you've just created a new, thinner, weaker butt section. Resist this temptation.

When a fish jumps, give it slack by dropping the tip of your rod. This is a technique used in fishing for tarpon which are known for their athletic leaps. This move has been nicknamed "bowing to the king."

If a fish decides to run, let it run. Before it happens, make sure your reel drag is properly set. Trying to reset it after the fact is not easy. If your reel has an exposed rim, you can try palming it to create some resistance and tire the fish out.

Take charge! Control the fish. Theodore Gordon, known as "the father of American dry fly fishing" once said, "There is no more pitiful a sight than a grown man being controlled by a fish." I agree.

Landing The Fish

Whether you release or creel your fish, you still need to land it properly so you'll be able to handle it. Reel or strip the fish in to about a foot before the end of the fly line. **Do not bring the fly line in past the tip top.**

Now lift the tip of the rod toward you to bring the fish closer. If you're going to net the fish, bring it to the net by using the rod. Don't try to chase the fish with the net. Try to maneuver the fish over the net with your rod and then simply lift the net in order to net the fish.

The same technique applies if you intend to release the fish, only instead of netting the fish you need to keep enough tension on the line so that you can grab hold of the hook. Take the hook by the shank and turn it upside down. If it is barbless or the barb has been crushed down, the fish should come right off. You may need to use a pair of hemostats, pliers or hook-releasing device to help accomplish this.

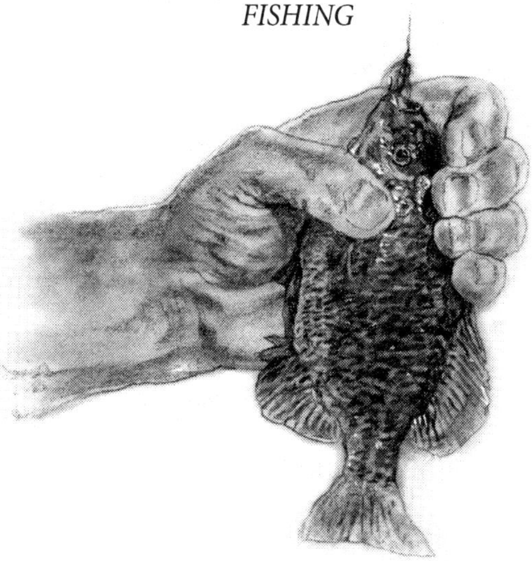

Handling A Sunfish

It's preferable to release the fish while it's in the water. If the fish is small, you can just lift it out of the water and swing it toward you. If it's a panfish or some other species with sharp-spined dorsal fins, cup your hand and move it down over the fish so you can compress those spines as you hold it.

> ***Safety Tip***
>
> *Although it's unlikely to catch a catfish on a fly, it sometimes happens. If it happens to you, stay away from its spines! They are poisonous!*

Whenever you need to use two hands to do any of these tasks, simply bring your rod diagonally across your chest and secure it in the inside crook of the elbow of your "line hand." Now your rod will be held still with some slack line and you'll have both hands free.

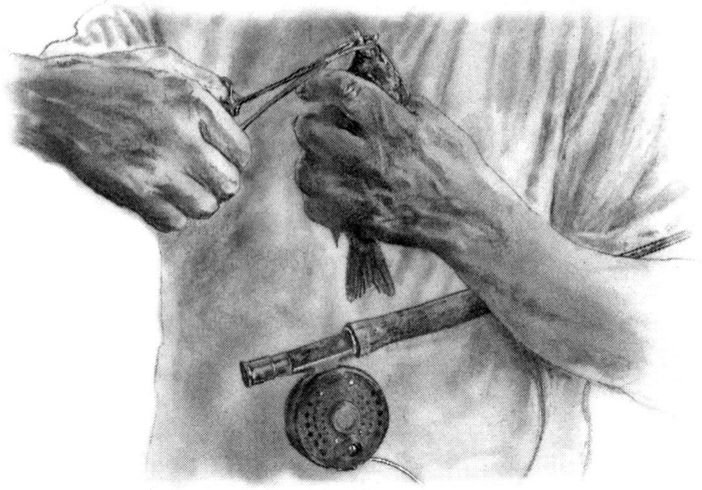

Releasing The Fish

Sometimes releasing a fish is just a matter of taking the hook out and putting it back in the water as described above. Other times, it's a little more involved.

If the fish is hooked hard, use your hemostats to remove the hook. If you still can't remove it, cut the fly off and release the fish with the fly still in it. The hook will rust out in a short time and you'll do less damage to the fish.

If it looks as though the fish is having a hard time when you place it in the water, it may need some help. Hold the fish gently and position it facing the current until it swims away on its own. If you're in stillwater, move the fish forward and back to help revive it.

The reason for doing this is to give the fish more oxygen. When the fish is stressed out from battle, it builds up lactic acid in its system and this prevents its intake of oxygen.

If too much lactic acid builds up in the fish's system, it may die even after it is released. If you kill and eat it, too much lactic acid will make it taste bad.

These are good reasons to try not to stress out the fish too much. To prevent this, do not overplay your fish and try not to fish with equipment which is too light. Trying to increase your sport at the expense of the fish is really very unsportsmanlike behavior.

Fish have a protective coating of slime. Handling disturbs the fish's slime coat and renders it more susceptible to disease. Try to handle the fish as little as possible. If you must handle it, wet your hands first.

Try to keep the fish in the water as much as possible, especially during cold weather when their gills can freeze if exposed to the air.

If you want to photograph your catch, be prepared so you can snap a picture and get the fish back in the water as soon as possible.

There are still no real solid statistics on how many fish survive after they're released. Even if your intent is the noblest in the world, if you stress the fish out too much or handle it too roughly, then the fish not only dies but is wasted as well.

Lately, catch-and-release has become fashionable. There is no doubt that in most cases this practice is a wonderfully effective conservation method, but there are times when it's appropriate and even beneficial to creel fish. "Put-and-take" programs are created where trout, which are coldwater fish, are introduced into warmwater lakes or ponds during the autumn. They can survive through the winter and into the early spring, but will die when the water heats up in later spring and summer. In this case, it makes sense to kill your limit of fish, since they're looking at a death sentence anyway.

Under certain conditions, conservation authorities determine that some fish should be culled from that body of water for the benefit of that resource. In this case, it's obviously correct to kill your limit, and may even be wrong or counterproductive to release them.

I personally feel that native fish (fish that are indigenous to their environment) are a precious commodity and should be preserved by releasing them. There are some exceptions, such as saltwater species that are known at the time to have abundant populations.

It is our responsibility to keep informed, to make intelligent decisions, and to be reasonable in regard to the amount of fish kept.

Catch-and-release can have a great benefit on a fishery, but should not be followed as blind dogma.

Killing Fish

At those times when killing fish is appropriate, it should be done quickly and as humanely as possible. The best way to dispatch a fish is to strike it on the top of the head. This can be done with a small club which the British in their typical dry humor have christened a "priest."

It is cruel and irresponsible to let an animal die slowly. Stringers are torture devices which only serve to keep a fish stressed out for hours and hours, which in turn creates lactic acid within their system and results in tainted meat.

Native Brook Trout

Bluefish

SPORTSMANSHIP

In my opinion, the most important qualification for being a true sportsman is being a conservationist. Sportsmanship deals with the behavior of those engaged in sports. With most sports, this concerns behavior toward other people. With sports that deal with nature as well as other people, it also concerns behavior toward the resource itself. This means conservation.

The ideal pattern is this: first you learn to love fishing. Then you learn to love the fish. Next, you learn to love and respect the habitat which enables the fish to exist. Then finally, you take some action to protect the habitat and therefore the fish.

Some people skip a couple of steps and go right to becoming stewards of the environment. Some suffer from some sort of arrested development and never get beyond the fishing. This is a shame, not only because the environment can use all the help it can get, but also because conservation practices and involvement have their own rewards.

If you're ever involved in a clean-up or restoration which turns an abused or neglected resource back to the way it's supposed to be, or a campaign which prevents a place or a species from becoming destroyed, you'll understand just how wonderful that can make you feel.

There are three basic ways to support conservation: financial contributions, hands-on involvement such as clean-up and restoration, and political activism.

The best and easiest way to participate is to join a conservation organization. There are many great ones out there. I belong to Trout Unlimited and the Coastal Conservation Association. There are many more, all dedicated and effective. Added benefits from joining these organizations are the new friends you make and the great fishing information you pick up from your fellow members.

It's all pretty basic. You can't go fishing without fish. (Actually you can, but it kind of limits your opportunities for catching them.) Conservation is both an insurance for, and an investment in, the future of the sport, not to mention the planet.

How we relate to the fish and the environment is one aspect of sportsmanship. The other part is how we behave towards other people. The subject of fishing courtesy has been discussed and written about extensively. I can't understand why. To me, it's all pretty simple. Courtesy is something that parents should teach their children. The rest is just common sense. If you see someone fishing and you have the slightest hint you're infringing on their area, ask them. If you're lucky enough to be the first one to score at a great spot, have some fun, then let the other guy have a good time, too.

Throughout this book, I've come down rather hard on the elitist attitude that pervades fly fishing. Traditionally, fly fishing has been a gentlemen's sport and when it comes to gentlemanly behavior, I'm in full agreement with this tradition. To put it bluntly, any slob can catch fish, but a fisherman who conducts himself as a gentleman is a true sportsman.

Bonefish

SAFETY

When you become involved with any outdoor activity, you soon realize that there may be a certain degree of danger involved.

Nature is a powerful force, capricious and often unpredictable. At any time a situation can turn ugly. At any moment something seemingly benign can turn around and bite you in your proverbial behind.

Abrupt weather changes, thunderstorms, currents and tides, fast moving streams, hidden deep spots, loose rocks, etc. can turn a pleasant day of sport into a nightmare.

Of course its true that there's danger everywhere. Fatal accidents occur at home and probably the most dangerous place you can be is behind the wheel of your car.

Nevertheless, there's something particularly upsetting about having an activity which is supposed to provide fun and relaxation turn sour. Most of these situations can be prevented or alleviated by proceeding with **caution**. Safety is about **common sense and being prepared.**

Know the situation you're getting into. Ask about any place you've never been to before. Seek information. It will not only help insure your safety but it can also increase your chances of successful fishing. Listen to weather reports. Try to equip yourself properly, especially in terms of clothing, water and food. Tell someone where you're going and when you expect to be back. Don't rely on your cell phone to call for help. You could be in a dead zone, or your battery could lose its charge.

Always wear a hat and sunglasses to protect youself from both the sun and from being hit in the face by a fly from a badly aimed back cast.

Above all, **don't take unnecessary chances.** We all get caught up in the excitement of the moment. We all want to catch fish, but remember there's no fish in the world worth hurting yourself or dying for.

Shoshin – Beginner's Mind

SOME FINAL THOUGHTS

In Zen Buddhism there is a concept called "Shoshin" which means "beginner's mind." Shoshin celebrates the attitude of the beginner bringing a freshness, an eagerness and an open mind to a new endeavor. It is a quality that one tries to maintain even as one becomes more experienced and proficient in that endeavor.

The enthusiasm and the excitement generated when first starting out is something that will never take place on that great a scale again. Beginning the fly fishing experience is something to be savored and cherished.

Learning is a process that continues as you explore the sport. After a while, you begin to realize that the learning part is the fun part. And since more learning takes place in the beginning, being a beginner is the most fun.

In fly fishing, the learning process takes place on a couple of different fronts. We learn by studying the experts. Volumes of incredible knowledge and advice have been written on fly fishing. Even reading enough to give you a fundamental background in the literature of fly fishing is a scholar's task, but it's all there for you to select from and pursue on whatever level you choose.

Taking that knowledge to the water and testing it out to see how it works for you is the next step. Remember, what is gospel on one body of water might be useless on another. This is where trial-and-error becomes your greatest teacher. This is where "beginner's mind" counts. Put this into practice and eventually you'll develop your own strategies and become your own expert.

Lastly and most importantly, don't take fly fishing too seriously. It's just fishing, not a religion. Relax and enjoy it and above all, remember to have fun!

FURTHER READING AND RESOURCES

Books

Rosenbauer, Tom. *The Orvis Fly-Fishing Guide.*
New York, NY: Nick Lyons Books, 2007.
A great intermediate book.

Krieger, Mel. *The Essence of Flycasting.*
San Francisco, CA: Club Pacific, 2006.
A step-by-step, well-illustrated casting guide.

McNally, Bob. *Bob McNally's Complete Book of Fishermen's Knots, Fishing Rigs, And How To Use Them.*
Jacksonville, FL: McNally Outdoor Productions, 1993.
More knots than you'll ever need to know about, with clear, easy-to-follow illustrations.

Hughes, Dave. *Handbook of Hatches.*
Mechanicsburg, PA: Stackpole Books, 1987.
A clear presentation of the insects trout feed on and the flies that match them.

Hughes, Dave. *American Fly Tying Manual.*
Portland, OR: Frank Amato Publications, 2000.
Even if you don't want to venture into fly tying, this book is an excellent reference for understanding and identifying flies.

Leiser, Eric and Vinciguerra, Matt.
Orvis Guide to Beginning Fly Tying.
Bennington, VT: Abenaki Publishers Inc, 1993.
If you want to learn to tie flies, this is a great place to start. It is written by two great fly tiers of the famous Catskill school.

Schullery, Paul. *Royal Coachman.*
New York, NY: Simon & Schuster, 1997.
Fly fishing history and personal reflection at its best.

Clemens, Dale P. ***Fiberglass Rod Making.***
South Hackensack, NJ: Stoeger Sportsman's Library, 1974.
Don't let the title or the date fool you. The rod building information in this book is highly applicable to building today's graphite rods. The small amount of information not covered is made up for by the presentation of some techniques from the past that have been long overlooked.

Websites

All About Fly Fishing
http://about-flyfishing.com
This site contains a large number of articles on various fly fishing topics.

Beginning Fly Tying
http://www.flyanglersonline.com/flytying/beginners
A well-organized site with clear instructions and excellent visuals. A section of the flyanglers.com site.

Graphite Rod Building
http://flyanglersonline.com/begin/graphite
Another section of the flyanglers.com site, also well presented and thorough.

A Fly Fishing History by Dr. Andrew N. Herd
http://www.flyfishinghistory.com
A well-constructed site that covers the history of fly fishing from its origins to the present.

Periodicals

These magazines may be purchased at most newsstands or you can order them online.

American Angler
http://www.americanangler.com

Fly Fisherman
http://www.flyfisherman.com

Fly Rod & Reel
http://www.flyrodreel.com

Internet Radio

AskAboutFlyFishing.com
http://www.AskAboutFlyFishing.com
A bimonthly internet radio show hosting fly fishing experts discussing and taking questions about their areas of expertise. Catch the show in real time to ask questions directly or listen to their archives.

INDEX